THE BUFALINO
MAFIA CRIME FAMILY

The Complete History of a Northeastern Pennsylvania Criminal Organization

MAFIA LIBRARY

© **Copyright 2023 - All rights reserved.**

The content contained within this book may not be reproduced, duplicated or transmitted without direct written permission from the author or the publisher.

Under no circumstances will any blame or legal responsibility be held against the publisher, or author, for any damages, reparation, or monetary loss due to the information contained within this book, either directly or indirectly.

Legal Notice:

This book is copyright protected. It is only for personal use. You cannot amend, distribute, sell, use, quote or paraphrase any part, or the content within this book, without the consent of the author or publisher.

Disclaimer Notice:

Please note the information contained within this document is for educational and entertainment purposes only. All effort has been executed to present accurate, up to date, reliable, complete information. No warranties of any kind are declared or implied. Readers acknowledge that the author is not engaged in the rendering of legal, financial, medical or professional advice. The content within this book has been derived from various sources. Please consult a licensed professional before attempting any techniques outlined in this book.

By reading this document, the reader agrees that under no circumstances is the author responsible for any losses, direct or indirect, that are incurred as a result of the use of the information contained within this document, including, but not limited to, errors, omissions, or inaccuracies.

TABLE OF CONTENTS

Introduction 1

Chapter 1 : Northeastern Pennsylvania's Unique History 5

Industrial Background, Immigration History, And Economic Developments 5

Cultural And Social Factors That Shaped The Region's Identity And Dynamism 8

The Historical Events And Eras That Led To The Rise Of Organized Crime 9

Socioeconomic Issues That Influenced Criminal Behavior 12

The Bigger Picture Of Organized Crime In The United States And How It Varies By Area 13

Formation And Collaboration Of Northeastern Pennsylvania's Criminal Networks And Organizations 16

Chapter 2 : The Bufalino Family's Origins 19

Roots And Migration To The United States 19

The Bufalino Crime Family Before Bufalino 22

    The Men From Montedoro 22

    The Rise Of John Sciandra 25

During The Same Years: A Glimpse To The Mafia Central Luciano-Genovese-Costello Alliance 27

Chapter 3 : The Rise Of Russell Bufalino 29

    Russell Bufalino's Mentor: Stefano Magaddino 29

    Bufalino Begins The Northeastern Pennsylvania Conquest 33

    The Fearless Min Matheson Puts Bufalino In Trouble 34

    Bufalino's Grasp On The Teamsters Union 37

    Bufalino Keeps Rising 39

Chapter 4 : Criminal Enterprises Take Shape 43

    Cuba Business 43

    Loan-Sharking 47

    Infiltration Into Labor Unions 48

    Extortion 52

    A Characteristic Gangster: The "Irishman" 53

Chapter 5 : Law Enforcement's Involvement 57

    Becoming Nationwide Famous In The Wrong Way: The Apalachin Meeting 57

        Origins Of The Apalachin Meeting 58

        The Apalachin Meeting Fiasco And Its Consequences 61

    The Bufalino Crime Family Targeted By Law Enforcement ... 62

        Techniques To Combat Organized Crime 64

        Informants And Witnesses 65

    Federal Bureau Of Investigations Vs. Russell Bufalino 67

    Women And Sports 69

Chapter 6 : The Tenacity And Adaptability Of The Bufalino Family 73

    The Struggle For The Teamsters' Control 73

Hoffa Goes Out Of Control 81
Time Magazine Convinces Bufalino He Has Had Enough 83

Chapter 7 : The Bufalino Family In Intriguing And Mystery Stories Of National Interest (And Beyond) 87
Russell Bufalino And *The Godfather* 87
The Truth About Jimmy Hoffa's Disappearance 91
Related To Jfk's Assassination? 94

Chapter 8 : The Disintegration 97
The Strange End Of An Era 97
Russell Bufalino Finally In Jail 98
The Bufalino Crime Family After Bufalino 104

Conclusion 107

Glossary 111

References 119

INTRODUCTION

It would be very difficult to find a Mafia history reader or a person interested in organized crime who hasn't watched and loved Francis Ford Coppola's classic film *The Godfather* and its sequels. However, only a few know that legendary actor Marlon Brando's performance in the movie was in great part inspired by a real Mafia boss of those times: Russell Bufalino.

Marlon Brando actually met and hung out with Russell Bufalino during the making of *The Godfather*, and some of the actors who played in the film were real gangsters outside of the set. The real Mafia was similar to the set of the iconic movie that defined the way we imagine the Mafia, its leaders, and hitmen during its heyday in America during the 1950s, 1960s, and beyond.

But how did Russell Bufalino end up on *The Godfather*'s set with Francis Ford Coppola and Marlon Brando? And before that, how did he end up being one of the most prominent mob leaders in the United States?

The Bufalino crime family's history began before it was named the "Bufalino family" and even before Russell Bufalino came to the United States from his native land in Montedoro, Sicily. In fact, it began before he was born. The story presented in the following pages and chapters begins with the origins of American organized crime when the original and authentic Mafiosi came to the United

States from Sicily and South Italy between the late 19th and the early 20th century. It goes on with the formation of Italian-American crime families in the various regions and cities of the United States. And it arrives at organized crime's golden era and its fall to our time.

We will begin this journey by studying and comprehending the broader historical, social, and economic context of Northeastern Pennsylvania and, more generally, of the early to mid-20th century United States. What was the industrial background, economic basis, and development of the Pennsylvania region inside the growing new superpower of the world? And how this growth made the United States and Northeastern Pennsylvania attractive to immigrants from Europe, and especially Italy and Sicily. We'll see how the cultural and social factors of the region, along with immigration, are related to the birth and rise of organized crime and how the latter varied by area in the United States.

With a clear historical vision, we'll continue entering the universe of the Italian-American Mafia, especially the Bufalino crime family, and its origins and roots: From the migration to the United States to the "Men of Montedoro" and the formation of organized crime in Northeastern Pennsylvania to the rise of Russell Bufalino. We'll meet Bufalino's mentors, like Stefano Magaddino, his competitors, and his rivals. We will learn about other rising mobsters and the fearless labor unionist Min Matheson, all while continuing to follow Bufalino's conquering of Northeastern Pennsylvania and beyond.

We will examine in detail the criminal enterprises and operations of the Bufalino family, from the majestic coasts of Havana in Cuba, that Las Vegas with the sea that didn't happen, to the brutal and raw typical activities of organized crime, such as loan-sharking, extortion, and infiltration in labor unions, to exploit businessmen and workers alike. We'll meet characteristic gangsters like Frank

Sheeran and notorious events of Mafia history, such as the infamous Apalachin Meeting, with its origins and consequences.

No criminal organization can go on growing without being subject to the attention of law enforcement, and the Bufalino crime family was no exception. We will see the Federal Bureau of Investigations target and take on the Bufalino family, using all the modern techniques and methods of those years spent battling against organized crime—from wiretaps and surveillance to witness protection programs and informants. We will see the efforts of the law to put an end to criminal activity and the capacity to persist and invent new ways to prolong it from the tenacious Bufalino and his crime family.

We will delve into the interconnection between legitimate and criminal syndicates, labor union leaders collaborating with Mafia bosses, and government officials determined to destroy organized crime or to accept it as a de facto working partner and ally—from Batista's Cuba and World War II United States to the times of John and Robert Kennedy and Richard Nixon.

Learn how Russell Bufalino, who was quiet, calm, and uninterested in displaying wealth or detaining official power, enlarged the Bufalino family's reach far beyond Northeastern Pennsylvania, its bases in the Pittston, Scranton, and Wilkes-Barre area, obtaining national status, while its boss was the leader of two more crime families.

Finally, read intriguing and shocking stories and rumors that involved the Bufalino crime family—from the aforementioned making of *The Godfather* to the mystery of labor union leader Jimmy Hoffa to the assassination of JFK, as a last glimpse of fascination before the chapter dedicated to the eventual and inevitable disintegration. The sad but just demise of a criminal empire that was more efficient than spectacular, and it, fortunately, left its place to a more advanced society, which does not need criminal methods to satisfy needs and desires and be effective—or so we hope. Was it thanks to the combined efforts of law enforcement and the government, or because time ultimately beats everything and everyone? Were the protagonists of the story finally caught off guard by law and civilized society, or did they just grow old and leave with their consciences intact, like Russell Bufalino after turning 90 years old?

It could be a little bit of both. The fact is that the history of the Bufalino crime family is a narrative of a past we would want to be gone forever. It is a testament to the pursuit of success and personal and family growth that can sometimes surpass the limits of law and social peace. Yet, at the same time, it's also a testament to the need for justice, transparency, cohesion, and truth in human societies. Ultimately, it is a captivating mystery and crime story that continues to attract researchers and readers interested in organized crime.

CHAPTER 1

NORTHEASTERN PENNSYLVANIA'S UNIQUE HISTORY

The late 19th and early 20th centuries were pivotal for Northeastern Pennsylvania's industrialization, with coal mining at its center. The industrial growth attracted immigration waves, which created distinct and vibrant ethnic local communities across the region. At the same time, the challenging conditions of labor and life produced intense labor struggles and a working-class ethos. However, the fractured cultural and social environments and economic difficulties provided the best ground for organized crime. The Prohibition era and the Great Depression, along with weak law enforcement, completed the puzzle, creating very advantageous times for Mafia growth.

Industrial Background, Immigration History, and Economic Developments

Undoubtedly, the late 19th and early 20th centuries were critical periods in Northeastern Pennsylvania's economic and social histories and the most defining ones until the mid-20th century. That period determined the area's industrialization and its importance for the modern industrial economy in the United

States. As in earlier cases and the British historical model, what was crucial for the development of Northeastern Pennsylvania was its significant coal reserves. This natural advantage made the area one of the most noteworthy places for coal mining and central to the broader establishment and growth of the American industry.

The region's economy proliferated following the general boom of the American economy, which quickly became one of the most industrialized nations on earth, soon to be the most industrialized and rich. Northeastern Pennsylvania's mines played the role held by rivers and lakes in the pre-industrial economy, securing the flourishing of production and social growth around them. Since the population constantly increased, local communities were founded and filled with homes, churches, and schools.

The industrialization of the United States proceeded in extraordinary rhythm, and so did the importance of Northeastern Pennsylvania's coal mines, which became even more prominent. That situation brought a corresponding socioeconomic development in the region, attracting always more people who wanted to work in the mines. So, the cities and towns in the area increased and grew more prominent. At the same time, the population was always more diverse, as coal mining was one of the jobs new immigrants and unqualified workers more often tended to do to make a living, along with working in related factories.

Northeastern Pennsylvania became a multinational and multicultural region as soon as the early 20th century, as thousands of Irish, Italians, and Eastern Europeans, like Polish, arrived massively in the area and began working in the mines and the factories. That fact made the region what we would call a melting pot, which used to have a negative meaning and now has instead a positive one, with populations from different cultural backgrounds that had to find and form common grounds and values. Or that's the way we would see it today. Historically, what happened was the formation of closed and knit communities aligned with the national heritage of the population, even though they were all Europeans, Christians, and working-class people.

Even more challenging for the immigrants than getting along with each other was dealing with the working conditions in the mines and factories, which were definitely much harsher than we could understand, looking at historical eras closer to our lifestyles and working habits. On the contrary, the initial periods of industrialization were extremely tough and rough for workers. They responded with many labor struggles, claiming better working conditions and, of course, bigger salaries.

In any case, Northeastern Pennsylvania's social and economic fabric was shaped by its position in the US industrial growth as a major coal resource in the country. That brought economic, social, and demographic growth destined to be overthrown around the mid-20th century. By then, the coal industry declined heavily, and the region stopped being a central point in the American economic process. Many mines and factories simply ceased to exist, and ever-growing communities slipped and lost their potential. The new condition drastically changed the region's economic situation, and people had to find solutions and transform their society to adapt.

In this context, organized crime would appear in Northeastern Pennsylvania, where the tight and closed communities formed in the previous decades of the immigrant flows would make the perfect social basis for activities of that kind.

Cultural and Social Factors That Shaped the Region's Identity and Dynamism

Northeastern Pennsylvania is a blue-collar region, no doubt about that. As mentioned, industrialization and coal mines were the essential elements of its social fabric from the economic point of view. In that sense, the working-class ethos could not be anything but prevailing. Factory workers and coal miners were the population's bulk and heart. Working hard and being down-to-earth became the dominant anthropological model for the area's people. That condition also brought a sense of companionship among the working class, forged by the various shared, sometimes really hard, struggles about the working conditions. Struggles, strikes, and difficulties gave rise to narratives of resilience, perseverance, and working together to overcome aversion.

The harsh socioeconomic conditions and the not-so-many opportunities made life difficult but also created an attitude of collective activism against adversities that has since culturally characterized local society. Also, values such as family and religion were central to the region's cultural identity, with churches being central places of socialization and moral guidance for the communities of Northeastern Pennsylvania.

Yes, but that was pretty much it. What was even more crucial and determined heavily social dynamics was the fact of the different national heritages. Common grounds proved to be less influential than the predominant element of ethnic origins, and essentially, the immigrant working population formed closed and tight-knit communities based on ethnicity. The Italians constructed Italian-American blocks and neighborhoods; the Irish formed Irish-American blocks and communities; the Polish created Polish-

American ones. Those ethnic-based communities were in great part culturally homogeneous and sometimes entirely homogeneous, as people continued to live according to the habits and customs of the country of origin, often spoke their national language instead of English, and had no intention of flowing and abandoning themselves into a multicultural melting pot.

Inside the national communities were shared cultural traditions but also the camaraderie of people who felt they had to deal with a quite strange or even hostile environment that did not conform with their own values and customs, or, to put it simpler, it did not speak their language.

The area's deindustrialization of the mid-20th century shocked the cultural and social format forged until then in Northeastern Pennsylvania. Historically and in the long term, it was not something terrible, as it led to a reshaping of local society, economy, and identity. The heavy landscape of the grey coal mines and factories of the first industrialization—forgive this caricatural image, just to make the point—gradually gave way to a more colorful landscape entering the era of advanced technology, better education and healthcare, and more opportunities. However, in the meantime, the osmosis of social, cultural, and economic conditions would produce social forms in the opposite historical direction, similar to those encountered in much older societies, such as mafia families.

The Historical Events and Eras That Led to the Rise of Organized Crime

We cannot escape evidence. Immigration was one of the principal historical factors of the United States' economic and social growth, but also one of the factors that led to the rise of organized crime in the United States in the early 20th century. As mentioned, the formation of totally inhomogeneous local societies, where different ethnicities had to coexist with their particular customs and traditions, resulted in a fractured cultural and social context. To make matters worse, economic difficulties, racism, and discrimination further increased the feeling of some communities that they had to find ways to survive and get more decadent on their own without integrating with the rest of society or without integrating wholly and harmoniously. That was an environment favorable to the development of groups living with norms outside official law, proposing themselves as forms of protection and support, especially to members of the same national community or, in other terms, minority.

However, the list of the historical events that led to the rise of organized crime is much longer. The rapid urbanization itself and, to be more precise, the inability of the state to create in a similarly quick manner law enforcement capable of dealing with the new dimensions of cities created a weakness in implementing the law and corruption. Often, law enforcement was not as strong as the situation demanded because there were insufficient resources, trained agents, organization, and coordination. The conditions were objectively very harsh, as a young state had to take care of an ever-growing and diverse population and social and cultural ambiance.

The young state was not totally innocent, though, as after thousands of years during which humans had used various alcoholic beverages, a US administration had the not-so-smart idea to prohibit alcohol in 1920. The Prohibition Era had a central role in the rise of organized crime, and we could say that it was the single most decisive event, as it created a very lucrative market, in that case, the black market, perfectly fit for rising criminal businesses or for the creation of new ones. On that occasion, notorious criminal organizations such as Chicago Outfit and the New York Five Families rose. They had the opportunity to take over the production and distribution of alcohol with illicit distilleries and bars and control the contraband. Finally, in 1933, the US administration canceled the Prohibition, eliminating the vast black market that had offered wealth to criminal groups, but dismantling them was not equally easy at that point.

Having established their organizations and expanded their activities in many other sections, criminal enterprises developed the ability to use political struggles and turmoil to their advantage, applying influence to politicians and labor unions, as well as exploiting other illegal activities, like illegal sports betting and gambling.

And then, there is another crucial historical event. The Great Depression, beginning in 1929, brought an economic and social earthquake with immeasurable consequences, which the criminal organizations were keen and able to use to their advantage. In desperate conditions, with difficulties making a living or even surviving, many people came close to organized crime in search of financial support. In that way, criminal organizations put down deeper roots in local societies, exploiting the favorable conditions offered by the abovementioned factors.

Socioeconomic Issues That Influenced Criminal Behavior

It's obvious, then, that socioeconomic issues had a critical influence on forming the social habitat in which criminal organizations found the opportunity to establish themselves and grow. If we want to take a closer look at them, we cannot omit the examination of the last factor mentioned in the previous paragraph, unemployment. The unemployment rates rose higher than ever after the Great Depression and before President Franklin D. Roosevelt's "New Deal." Still, in the case of Northeastern Pennsylvania, they were again at higher levels during the mid-20th century, as the coal industry declined, and many people lost what was, till then, their principal income source. Criminal organizations were eager to fill the gap before the growth of the normal economy could have by offering jobs in their illegal activities, like the ones already mentioned, or others like loan-sharking, forced protection, and raw blackmailing.

Also, the black markets formed during the failures of the regular economy or mistakes made by governments that alter the function of the market for the worse can be beneficial for organized crime to thrive. The aforementioned Era of Prohibition was an important example, but other market failures had similar results, such as the one imposed by the deindustrialization of Northeastern Pennsylvania. Not only unemployment but also the shrinking of the market itself, caused by the fall of the incomes and consumption of the population, created gaps in consumer goods that criminal organizations were able to cover through illegal channels. In that case, organized crime could also appear as welfare and earn the sympathy and social legalization of many people.

That kind of social legalization and sympathy was favored by another socioeconomic factor that played an important role in the rise of organized crime, which was economic inequality, especially in the Northeastern Pennsylvania region. Harsh working conditions of miners and low wages, in contrast with the wealth of the mine owners, created resentment and hate, as the working class felt it was a provocation and an injustice. Criminal organizations provided a sense of support and justice like law enforcement not controlled by the rich, whom poor workers often saw as the owners of the official law and the state. Related to this last factor was also the exploitation of labor struggles and disputes by criminal organizations, as they deftly infiltrated labor unions.

Unsurprisingly, these kinds of perceptions and activities empowered the roots and acceptance of criminal organizations in local and national close-knit communities that, since the beginning, were formed and came closer precisely in order to deal with substantial economic problems and insecurities. The result was that, in many cases, organized crime was perfectly integrated into the social fabric of communities and neighborhoods, justified and supported.

The Bigger Picture of Organized Crime in the United States and How It Varies by Area

The United States is a very big country and the biggest economy in the world for more than a century now. Organized crime in the United States could not be a simple and one-way thing. Complexity and differentiation between the various regions of the country are evident.

Wanting to paint the bigger picture of organized crime in the United States, we can begin with socioeconomic factors related to the previous paragraphs, such as the decline of the coal industry in Northeastern Pennsylvania. Similar evolution also intervened in many other Rust Belt regions, beginning in the 1950s. In many cases, the great industrial zone of the United States faced increasing difficulties and problems, such as unemployment, low wages, shortcomings, and poverty. In those regions, criminal organizations offered financial outlets by employing people in their illegal businesses.

Another theme already mentioned is the cultural and national background, which more precisely favored organized crime in cases where national communities had a heritage of similar social forms. It's not a secret that the Mafia was a thing in the Italian South decades before it immigrated to the United States and that other ethnic communities had their own traditions of organized crime, be it Hispanic, African, Asian, or anything else. Again, the fractured cultural and social fabric of the new country called the United States, combined with the material challenges and difficulties faced by the various communities, gave a hand to criminal traditions' rooting, at least in some of them.

There's no doubt, then, that organized crime varies between different local communities and regions. Yet, suppose we want to put things in relative order. In that case, we can locate and examine four mega-regions of the country, usually used for analysis, similar to those used by sports leagues' divisions: the East Coast, the Central or Midwest, the West Coast, and the South.

The East Coast, and especially the Northeastern part of it, where Pennsylvania is also located, is one of the most prominent candidates for the award of the region that has suffered most from organized crime. The Five Families in New York is a sharp reminder of the power that the Mafia had in the Big Apple, but other great cities on the East Coast, like the old NBA rivals Philadelphia and Boston, had their fair share. Drug distribution, raw extortion, and illegal gambling were some of the activities criminal organizations promoted in this deep urban area of the country, as elsewhere.

Then there is Chicago, in the central regions. "Chicago" had an almost mystical sense in the rest of the world, as it stood for something close to criminal utopia (or dystopia). Al Capone was a legendary name. Fortunately for the Windy City, the University of Chicago came with its famous School of Chicago in economics and social sciences. And, of course, Michael Jordan and the Chicago Bulls. However, during Prohibition, organized crime, especially the Chicago Outfit, had risen at an extraordinary rate in the city, influencing and corrupting politics and labor unions based on their profits from gambling, bootlegging, and more.

Moving to the West Coast, cinema has taken care of presenting the laundering and drug trafficking opportunities that criminal organizations can find in Los Angeles or the entertainment and gambling capital of the world, Las Vegas. The West Coast is not so related to classic Mafia, like Chicago and New York. Still, it has other types of organized crime, including Asian-American criminal organizations, cartels close to Latin American drug industries, and gangs.

Concluding the trip to the criminal side of the United States, the South, besides common activities like smuggling, bootlegging, drugs, motorcycle gangs, etc., is characterized by the presence of white-collar crime and elevated political corruption by organized crime.

Formation and Collaboration of Northeastern Pennsylvania's Criminal Networks and Organizations

Northeastern Pennsylvania summarized all the socioeconomic factors and the historical events that, as we saw, prepared the rise of organized crime in the United States. This region is the best example of the consequences of sudden economic holes, such as the unemployment and market shrinking caused by the Great Depression or the deindustrialization after the end of the coal industry era that we have mentioned on more occasions. It's also an excellent example of the role of ethnic differentiation in the formation of organized crime in the United States and the exploitation of labor struggles and unions.

But the most important and exciting is discovering the particular factors that made the region of Northeastern Pennsylvania a hub for organized criminal activities in the first place. That happened first during the 1920s and Prohibition because the area was perfect for contraband to supply New York, Philadelphia, and other nearby big cities with alcohol. Another geographical reason that made Northeastern Pennsylvania appealing to criminal organizations was the fact that the region offered opportunities to hide and escape more than others. There are rough terrains and woods where one can hide illegal operations and find ways out of law enforcement. That last one was not the strongest in the world in the early 20th century in the region, so we have another valid reason for criminal masterminds to set up their business, or departments of their business, in Northeastern Pennsylvania.

Geographical considerations are not finished yet, as the region presented another critical advantage, which was its nearness to some of the most important transportation arteries—a real treasure to criminal organizations and networks that looked for ways to enter or expand bootlegging enterprises. Obviously, the coal mining industry was in itself a very attractive element, as criminal organizations could and indeed did exploit part of the wealth produced, thereby infiltrating or racketeering labor unions or mine owners.

After organized crime was stabilized in the region thanks to all those geographical assets and took root in local communities, criminal organizations began to create networks with similar entities in nearby areas. The growing organizations, always having more resources and people at their disposal, now expanded in multiple communities, could then gain influence in bigger domains, like towns and also big cities. Collaboration with criminal organizations of other communities or cities multiplied the power of each of them, as they secured access to more resources, information, influence, and people in various sectors and professions. In that way, they were no longer locally limited organizations.

In this way, the criminal organizations made extended networks and alliances, could diversify their operations and businesses, and evolve in every aspect, rendering it more difficult for the authorities to confront and neutralize them. On the other hand, and even worse, the criminal networks had the ability to influence or control legitimate local businessmen, labor syndicates, and politicians.

The possibility of huge profits, offered by geography, natural resources, and position in the industrial and productive process, natural advantages. Those were the reasons for the formation and collaboration of criminal organizations and networks in Northeastern Pennsylvania. Gambling, drugs, contraband, controlling the black market and labor unions, loan-sharking, and raw extortion were all easier to think about and accomplish in Northeastern Pennsylvania's cultural, socioeconomic, and natural landscape.

CHAPTER 2
THE BUFALINO FAMILY'S ORIGINS

Russell Bufalino's family arrived in the United States, and he gained a reputation in local gangs in Buffalo, New York, as a teenager. A few years earlier, the Northeastern Pennsylvania crime family had been founded by the "Men of Montedoro." We'll see how the Northeastern Pennsylvania crime family's power and reach expanded with gangsters like John Sciandra and Joseph Barbara in leading roles as Bufalino began his criminal career. This chapter closes with a glimpse into the Lucky Luciano-Vito Genovese-Frank Costello alliance at the top of organized crime in the United States.

Roots and Migration to the United States

The Bufalino family was an Italian-American family from Sicily, the most oversized island of the Mediterranean, located in the Southern part of the Italian peninsula. Angelo Bufalino emigrated to the United States on July 9, 1903, to work as a coal miner. He settled in Pittston, Pennsylvania, where a broad Italian-American community was already sited. His wife Cristina Buccoleri and his kids would follow a few months later, arriving at New York's port in December 1903. Angelo Bufalino was the family's patriarch, but his role in our story is minimal. The founder of one of the most notorious crime families of the American 1900s was to become his son Russell.

Russell Alfred Bufalino was born Rosario Alfredo Bufalino on September 29, 1903, in Montedoro, Sicily, and that means he traveled to America with his mother and siblings when he was just two or three months old. This initial settlement would not last for long, though, as just a few months later, his father Angelo tragically died in a mine accident, like the ones that happened far more often than today in those harsh days of industrialization's first eras. Russell Bufalino's mother brought her children back to Sicily. Still, soon, she apparently understood that America offered more opportunities even without her husband, and she returned to the United States in January 1906.

The back and forth was not yet over for baby Russell, or better still, Rosario, as just four years later, he also lost his mother. Seven-year-old Buffalino was back in Sicily in 1910, only to finally return and settle in the United States on February 15, 1914. It was already a big tragic and adventurous story for a little boy, but what happened next would enter the books of organized crime's history.

When he was just 14 years old, Russell Bufalino left Pittston for Buffalo, New York. There, he would quickly follow the path of his criminal career, entering the local gangs of the Italian-American community as a teenager. He gained a growing reputation thanks to his ability to go unnoticed by the police and, in general, to his low profile, not attracting unwanted attention, attitude, and way of doing things. We can understand that he was really good at what he did, as around ten years later, on August 9, 1928, we find him getting married to the daughter of a traditional Mafia family from Sicily, Carolyn Sciandra. His fellow collaborators were often capable, too. Many later became leaders of powerful Mafia families of the East Coast and the Buffalo crime family.

The Bufalino family story, before it became the Bufalino crime family, is typical for the numerous Italians and other immigrants who flowed to the United States between the late 19th century and the early 20th century. Some of them worked hard for some years, then returned to their countries with packages full of money and founded their businesses back home (who knows if they were successful). Others stayed forever and became Americans. Their descendants are the Americans of today. A few of them were involved in crime and organized crime or brought it with them from their country of origin, and if we want to talk about the original Mafia, from Italy, South Italy.

The typical Italian immigrant, like Angelo Bufalino, settled in industrial areas of the United States to work in manual labor, as a worker in factories, construction jobs, and, in this case, mining. It's easy to understand that people in Italian communities, like in other immigrant communities, faced difficulties and challenges of every kind, from financial to cultural and social, and in some cases, discrimination, contempt, and racism. That, along with objective limits, such as not knowing the English language, made the immigrants form close-knit communities and neighborhoods, where they supported one another and lived according to their own cultural costumes and social norms. Mafia was one of them, in the case of Southern Italians and Sicilians.

The Bufalino family may have been exposed to the Mafia world back in Sicily before emigrating to America. Still, they had nothing to do with that when Angelo Bufalino decided to emigrate to the United States to work as a coal miner. Yet, others were traditional Mafia families all along, and they had a crucial role in the criminal careers of young immigrants with no support, parents, or future, like Rosario Bufalino, Americanized as Russell. Mafia's loyalty and support code, the sense of belonging to an organization, a hierarchical structure that would be by your side in any case if you were loyal to it, the feeling of being part of a *familia*, a family, could be attractive for many young Italian immigrants. Knowing the story of Russell Bufalino's family, with the death of both his parents when he was just a little boy, understanding the Mafia's appeal to him may become even more accessible.

The Bufalino Crime Family Before Bufalino

The Men From Montedoro

The criminal organization, often called the "Bufalino crime family," was founded long before Russell Bufalino was involved with organized crime. In fact, its history began when Bufalino was a baby and had just arrived for the first time in the United States. That's why the same crime family is also called by other names: Pittston crime family, Scranton and Wilkes-Barre crime family, Northeastern Pennsylvania Mafia, and more. The point is that it's not about a family in the biological sense of the word but about a criminal syndicate formed in those locations, which Russell Bufalino would lead only decades later.

Our story begins again in 1903, but this time, it's not about the Bufalinos from Montedoro in Sicily, who emigrate to the United States. This time is about people who were there already, and in those years began their criminal activity, Mafia style.

Tomasso Petto, "The Ox," was around 26 years old when he was murdered on October 21, 1905, in Browntown, a village near Pittston and Wilkes-Barre in Pennsylvania. He had been the best hitman of the Morello crime family. The Morello family was a criminal clan from Sicily, located in the early 1900s Manhattan, and Petto lived in Brooklyn. The Morellos were ruthless and used the most brutal methods of Cosa Nostra. They used to kill members of rival families without hesitation, put them in barrels, and leave them near the streets in order to shock and show who's the boss in the neighborhood.

Petto became notorious to the authorities, and on April 15, 1903, detectives from the New York Police Department arrested him for murder only after he put up a gunfight. They transferred him to the New York Central Jail, but he was released after an incredible mistake made by jail officials. And, of course, he left New York immediately, thanking his good luck. He went as far as he could, settling down where he could find people who could understand him and work together. That was Scranton in Pennsylvania, where he became a member of a local gang that operated in the extortion sector. A typical Mafia and Camorra mode, *Mano Nera*, Black Hand, meant extortion through intimidation, threatening kidnapping or violence, and life threats. Black Hand originated from the Kingdom of Naples back in the 1750s and entered the United States in the 1880s, next to Italian immigrants. But make no mistake, the victims of Black Hand were almost always other Italian immigrants, the non-criminal great majority, and especially the most successful and affluent ones.

Petto was finally killed in 1905, allegedly by a relative of one of his victims, but that didn't stop the crime family of Northeastern Pennsylvania from growing. The central figures were Steven Joseph La Torre, born Stefano, and Santo Volpe, who both came from Montedoro in Sicily, the home of the Bufalinos. La Torre founded what would later take the name "Bufalino crime family."

Born on March 12, 1886, La Torre emigrated to the United States and precisely in Pennsylvania in May 1903. In the immediate next years, the young Sicilian established criminal activities and soon saved enough money to cover the cost of his brother-in-law Mafia boss Santo Volpe's travel to America in 1906. This is a clear case of Mafia export, in which the criminal activity is transported to the United States from where it already existed and not created in the United States. Next, La Torre and Volpe founded an organization called "The Men from Montedoro," but in April 1907, they were arrested together with twenty other persons after they tried to sell protection to miners. One of the men who got arrested with the two young bosses from Montedoro was Charles Bufalino, uncle of Russell Bufalino, who by that time was still enjoying his soon-to-be lost mom's hugs as a three-year-old boy.

In 1908, Volpe became the boss of the newborn Italian-American criminal organization in Pittston, with La Torre's agreement, perhaps because he was more experienced. Born in 1880, he was a little bit older and had also been nurtured at the original Mafia school in Sicily. Known as the King of the Night, Volpe directed the crime family in Northeastern Pennsylvania successfully, as it got more prominent over time. The fact that he was a capable manager can be seen in that he somehow also became president of a coal company in the then-leading mining region of the United States. The intersection between the Mafia, coal industry, and labor unions is beginning to emerge while we try to examine those initial decades of organized crime.

The Volpe years as leader of the Northeastern Pennsylvania Mafia include the Prohibition Era, during which, as more times mentioned, those kinds of criminal organizations had the golden opportunity to expand their businesses. However, by the end of

Prohibition in 1933, we can see Volpe appointed as the new boss of the family John Sciandra after Volpe was suspected of murder. Wanting to protect the family, Volpe chose to operate from the background from now on, as, like said before, he had a very important legitimate occupation, too. From that position, behind the scenes, the "King of the Night" would have the role of advisor and mentor, also expanded until Russell's Bufalino rise, which we'll see later.

The Rise of John Sciandra

John Sciandra, born Giovanni Sciandra, arrived with his parents and siblings in the United States in 1908 when he was nine years old. He, too, was from Montedoro in Sicily. His criminal career began in the early 1920s after he moved to Pittston from Buffalo, New York, the place his family had settled when they first came. Sciandra went to Pennsylvania to work as a miner in the coal industry; no surprise there. But soon, he met the local crime family run by Volpe. He felt that bootlegging, bullying, and threatening were a better fit for his talents and interests than working buried inside the earth with his face choked in dust, and during the following years, he became one of the top executives of the local Italian Mafia.

BY 1933, Sciandra was the organization's leader, after Santo Volpe and next to Angelo Polizzi and Joseph Barbara. Then Volpe decided to retire to the background and appointed him the new boss. At the same time, Polizzi became the *consigliere*—the chief advisor of the family, as the Italian-Americans kept calling them.

During Sciandra's leadership in the 1930s, the Northeastern Pennsylvania crime family related closer to the more prominent Luciano-Genovese family of New York and operated under the latter's guidance. Sciandra remained the boss in Pittston until September 11, 1949, when he died of natural causes at the age of 50. It was then that Russell Bufalino became the boss of the soon-to-be-called Bufalino crime family after him.

We should talk more about the role of Joseph Barbara, who was born Giuseppe Barbara in Sicily in 1905. As said, he was one of the four leaders of the crime family in the Pittston and Scranton region. Some historians believe Barbara became the boss around 1940 after Sciandra was murdered. In fact, evidence shows that Sciandra was not murdered, and he maintained his leadership until his natural death in 1949. Barbara was *capodecina*—leader of a fraction of a family in the Buffalo crime family under the boss Stefano Maggadino, and he was close to the Pittston and Scranton crime family. His role was presumably overestimated because he hosted the infamous Apalachin meeting in 1957, which we will talk about later, and other meetings between members of the Italian Mafia in 1956-57 on his estate in Apalachin country. But that happened because Magaddino ordered him to host them because of the convenient location, not because Barbara was the boss.

The "Men from Montedoro," or more straightforward, the Italian-American criminal organization of the Pittston, Scranton, and Wilkes-Barre area, is what later evolved in the "Bufalino crime family." We do not have every detail on the succession, the structure, or the unfolding of the early events, and, of course, every criminal act. We must not forget we are talking about criminal actions that their protagonists, even many decades later, are unwilling to communicate with precision, as it can always be dangerous for them or members of their families and their businesses. Moreover, that kind of organization seldom has written documents and archives, as everybody can easily understand, and facts are transmitted through time in their internal circles and, generally, the broader communities by voice. However, we can suppose with certainty that the "Men from Montedoro" were involved in a lot of extortion, loan-sharking, and contraband of alcohol during Prohibition, as well as illegal gambling and other criminal activities.

It is also evident that over time, the organization's operations developed and enlarged to include broader areas and activities. The initial small group of young Sicilian immigrants grew and came in contact with other Italian-American crime families from other cities, like Buffalo.

During the Same Years: A Glimpse to the Mafia Central Luciano-Genovese-Costello Alliance

In the early 1920s, Lucky Luciano, Vito Genovese, and Frank Costello had formed an alliance that grew considerably in power during Prohibition and had the opportunity to develop various other activities, like illegal gambling and prostitution. Their power increased, and they had precise roles between them, as for what each of them contributed to the group. Luciano became the leader of the Commission, and Genovese was his second in command, while Costello was his consigliere. Luciano and Genovese were the classic charismatic and ruthless mob leaders, while Costello was able to secure political and judicial cover, contacting and bribing with a lot of money politicians and judges, as well as police officials. Others had more operational roles, like Albert Anastasia, who became the leader of the "Murder Incorporated." That was the name of the brutal homicidal group that executed many killings ordered by the Commission.

Lucky Luciano had named Vito Genovese the boss of one of the five families of New York. When Luciano was convicted for pandering in 1936, he appointed Genovese as the leader of the Commission, although temporarily. Lucky Luciano had not considered that Genovese had his own problems with the law and that his condition was equally precarious because of a murder in 1934, for which he was indicted.

Genovese went to Italy to be sure that he'd avoid getting into jail and found his motherland in an interesting situation. Those were the years of Benito Mussolini and Fascism's peak, and Genovese did leave the opportunity to go away from his hands. He became a Mussolini supporter and got every advantage he could. However, things didn't turn out very well for the Duce and Fascism, as we know. Genovese, with the admirable opportunism that a real gangster must always have, remembered his American patriotism and became an interpreter of the Allies after they landed in Italy in 1943. At the same time, exploiting his proximity to the US Army, he was stealing supplies and food from the army's trucks to sell them in the black market to the American and British soldiers. We know he did so because the Military Police arrested him. But the army had more important things to do than spending time with little thieves, so they didn't put him on trial.

That wasn't the case sometime later when he returned to the United States. Finally, he was about to be tried by the court for the murder that had happened in 1934. But the trial never happened, as the key witness died poisoned while taking medication.

Meanwhile, Frank Costello had risen to become the undisputed boss, as his more flexible and political way of doing things proved to be very efficient and earned him and the family a lot of money.

CHAPTER 3
THE RISE OF RUSSELL BUFALINO

Russell Bufalino rose from a local low-level gangster to a high-ranking Mafia boss on a national level. Bufalino's mentor, Stefano Magaddino, the historical boss of the Buffalo crime family, was a central figure in this rise. We'll see Bufalino learning a lot from Magaddino and becoming a respected member of the Magaddino family, for then marries Carolyn "Carrie" Sciandra, sister of the soon-to-be boss of the Northeastern Pennsylvania boss John Sciandra. The two bosses moved him to Northeastern Pennsylvania, where he grew more as a mobster, and he focused on labor racketeering and the garment industry. At the beginning of the 1950s, Bufalino was the most powerful boss in the region, so the FBI had to prepare its first report dedicated to him. Meanwhile, though, the fearless figure of labor unionist Miss Min Matheson gave problems to the Bufalino crime family

Russell Bufalino's Mentor: Stefano Magaddino

During the 1920s, Russell Bufalino learned much about being a successful gangster from one of the best, Stefano Magaddino. And just like every talented individual who's also intelligent enough to carefully attend the example of experienced mentors and learn from them, he always became more prominent. His rise began in the

Magaddino family's internal, as the boss appreciated his skills and attitude. Dealing successfully with the crime family's enemies, Bufalino gained Magaddino's respect, making his way as a new official member of the clan.

Stefano Magaddino historically led the Italian-American crime family in Buffalo, which, for that reason, is also called the Magaddino crime family. Magaddino was born in Sicily, in Castellammare del Golfo, on October 10, 1891. He immigrated to the United States when he was still very young, ten or eleven years old, and settled in Buffalo, in the western part of the state of New York. There, he was quickly involved in illegal activities and gradually elevated his status as a mobster in the area, gaining positions in the organized crime hierarchy in New York and nationally.

By the early 1900s, Magaddino entered and soon became the leader of the Italian-American criminal clan in the area. The clan, similarly to the "men from Montedoro" clan, was formed by men who originated from Castellammare del Golfo. Magaddino partnered with another clan, that of the Bonnano brothers, Giuseppe and Stefano, and soon after, they entered into a conflict with the Buccellato Mafia family, which was already established in the area. Stefano and Giuseppe were murdered, and their younger brother avenged their deaths by killing members of the Buccellato clan. Magaddino participated in that gang war, and in March 1917, he was the mastermind behind the killing of Felice Buccellato, the boss of the Buccellatos, based in Detroit.

In the early 1920s, Magaddino became the boss of the Italian-American crime family in Buffalo and would stay in that role for circa 40 years. How he ended the boss in Buffalo is worth mentioning.

Bartolo Fontana was a barber and also a gangster, apparently not of the highest level, who in August 1921 turned himself in and confessed the murder of Camillo Caiozzo, who five years earlier in Sicily was involved in the murder of Magaddino's brother Pietro. According to Fontana, he had acted to avenge that killing as a member of a clan called "Good Killers," whose members originated from Castellammare del Golfo, and the clan had been responsible for other murders as well. For whatever reason, Fontana was convinced that he was about to be killed by the clan, and he not only turned himself in to the New York police but also agreed to participate in a covered operation. He came in contact with Magaddino, telling him he needed some money to leave New York—he had killed Caiozzo in Avon, New Jersey. Magaddino agreed and met him at Grand Central Station. He gave him $30, but right after that, a team of undercover policemen came out and arrested him. In the following days, four more mobsters were arrested.

Yet, the charges against Magaddino could not be supported, so he was released, and he immediately left New York and settled in Buffalo. There, he came in contact and entered the pre-existent Buffalo crime family, whose boss was Joseph DiCarlo. Already in the following year, 1922, DiCarlo died, and Magaddino, who had made his reputation as an elite gangster, was elevated to the post of the new Buffalo crime family.

As a Mafia boss, Magaddino is known for the caution with which he used to approach his criminal businesses, guiding his crime family in a careful and even conservative manner, preferring a low-profile style. At the same time, in the metropolis of New York City and Chicago, the Italian-American Mafia was anything but low-profile, with a bombastic approach that made the crime families of the big cities notorious in the United States and globally. On the contrary, with his cautious approach, Magaddino managed to keep law enforcement relatively away from his activities and crime family, on which he was also careful to have a tight grasp and control rigorously every operation and action. This is how he remained boss for three decades, without excessive pressure from the authorities and the law in that period or afterward. Magaddino was accused of involvement in numerous criminal acts and activities, but there was never enough legal evidence to be convicted.

That's although he was also a member of the Commission. That was kind of a confederation of Mafia families in the United States. The organization was created to coordinate the illegal activities of Italian-American crime families in order to avoid or diminish conflicts between them—something like the United Nations or the World Trade Organization of Organized Crime. Also, the Commission helped crime families join forces in various issues and activities, giving them national dimensions, like controlling or influencing labor unions or cooperating in the sector of gambling.

Magaddino was a constant factor in organized crime after Prohibition, just like during it. He was a permanent member of the Commission for all those years, and his organization continued to have interests in various places and sectors. The area of Scranton was a source of earnings for Magaddino, as he received tributes from there. Bufalino had a pivotal role in defending and promoting Magaddino's interests in the area, as he was responsible for the collection and deposit of the tributes to Magaddino.

One of the things Bufalino learned from Magaddino was not to show off and provoke with his wealth. He used to wear simple clothes, the car with which he used to go around was old, and he didn't live in a palace but in a nearly ordinary American home, a little ranch he had bought for $22,000. Another important thing Bufalino learned from Magaddino, as we saw, was to be tough and merciless with the enemies. Having around him a group of experienced killers was his way of dealing with the enemies.

Moving on to his 70s, Stefano Magaddino decided that after 30 years, it was time to retire as boss of the Buffalo crime family. In the early 1960s, he appointed as new boss his brother Peter and, consequently, his son Joseph Magaddino.

Bufalino Begins the Northeastern Pennsylvania Conquest

Russell Bufalino's resolve and capacity to quickly analyze situations and find solutions elevated his status inside the Magaddino crime family and in Buffalo's outlaw underworld in general, as he secured his position as Stefano Magaddino's trusted protégé. Magaddino's respect was crucial for Bufalino to grow as a mobster and get married. In fact, the family brought him close to the daughter of another known family from back home in Sicily. The bride was Carolyn Sciandra, whom Russell Bufalino married in 1928. Sciandra was the sister of John Sciandra, whom we met in the previous chapter, the soon-to-be boss of the Pittston and Scraton crime family, the one that originated from Montedoro, which by coincidence was the hometown of Bufalino too.

This last fact, along with his parenthood with Charles Bufalino, his uncle, and of course, his marriage to John Sciandra's sister, made the two bosses, Magaddino and Sciandra himself, move Russell Bufalino to Northeastern Pennsylvania, to be Sciandra's second in command. That happened in 1938, five years after Sciandra had become Northeastern Pennsylvania's don, as we saw in the previous chapter. The facade job of Bufalino would be auto mechanic at a bottling plant whose owner was Joseph Barbara, Canada Dry.

By 1940, Bufalino was focused on understanding and operating better in the infiltrating and racketeering labor unions sector of Mafia activities and also in expanding his businesses in the garment industry. By the end of World War II, he had indeed grown and was doing serious business in New York as well. He owned a restaurant on West 48th Street. The name of the restaurant was "Vesuvio," the name of the volcano near Napoli that had destroyed Pompey in 67 CE. He also owned many dress shops as well as jewelry shops, alone or in common with others. His jewelry shops were in the "Diamond District" in Manhattan, a very famous place at the time, on West 47th Street. Bufalino's businesses in Pennsylvania were much more extensive but fundamentally of the same nature as he was operating with success in the garment industry. And just like in his early mob years, Bufalino had no real problems with the authorities or the police. He could grow his activities with relative peace, away from great tensions.

That was about to change in 1945. In that year, he came to the Pittston and Wilkes-Barre area for the first time as a representative of the International Ladies' Garment Workers Union. Her name was Min Matheson, and her arrival would be a game-changer.

The Fearless Min Matheson Puts Bufalino in Trouble

Before that, very few shops in Pittston and surrounding areas were aligned with the Union, but by 1946, Matheson had made sensibility on the garments industry workers' rights, and the courage of the ladies who worked as sewing-machine operators increased exponentially. In that year, for the first time, a protest against a shop owned by Bufalino took place. Thirty workers participated, prompted by the energetic Matheson. It didn't go so well for Matheson and the protesters, as a number of people in the neighborhood attacked them with insults. Of course, mobsters of the Bufalino crime family threatened them Mafia-style, hanging guns. Nevertheless, Matheson and the women who decided to follow her in this struggle against the horrible working conditions of the garment industry in the region were tenacious. They held their ground, continuing the protests outside Bufalino's store for eight straight months.

Watching his bully tactics fail in this case, Bufalino adopted a more elaborate approach against this unexpected disruption. He put up another labor union, the Anthracite Needle Workers Association, controlled by himself. Of course, that didn't mean that the good old bully Mafia approach would not be helpful, too. As the initial number of workers who chose to become members of the Bufalino-held union was comprehensibly low, Bufalino's men made them recall that not so many years before, the crime family had dealt with the competition of Lori Dress in a resolute and efficient way: They smashed its two hundred sewing machines accompanying the firm out of the market. Note that the police and judiciary knew very well what had happened and that the Bufalino organization was responsible for the attack, yet nobody could touch Bufalino or his men.

The combined tactics of Bufalino succeeded in bringing far more workers into his puppet union as members. However, Matheson was unbent. She kept visiting workplaces, shops, and crafts, trying to convince women workers to enter the International Ladies' Garment Workers Union.

Bufalino was not the only gangster boss who was worried about Matheson's actions and saw their profits diminishing because of them. In 1949, there were forty-plus factories in union contracts thanks to Matheson, and that was nothing good for a number of Mafia bosses who held shops and factories in the region. Bosses like Albert Anastasia, besides Bufalino, were exposed to profit losses in their garment industry businesses because of Matheson's game-changing operations in Northeastern Pennsylvania. Things became even more uncomfortable for him after Matheson started working to unionize Anastasia's employees, who worked in a show he owned near Hazleton. At the same time, Matheson's brother, Will Lurye, was leading protests in a factory owned in part by Anastasia in New York, as he was connected to shops and factories both in Pennsylvania and New York.

That was too much for the Mafia boss. His clan's response was ruthless and bloody. Two of Anastasia's men blocked Lurye while he was talking in a public telephone booth and stabbed him many times with knives, killing him at the post. The victim of this horrible crime was a father of four, and he had followed his sister's occupation, joining as an organizer of the Union, although they paid him only $80, and his previous job as a presser earned him almost double the money. Both of them had followed their father's example and career, who was a union organizer himself. At the time of his son's murder, he was in hospital, and he died a week later.

But Anastasia did not achieve what he had hoped for. Matheson did not abandon her mission, but on the contrary, she was more galvanized after her brother's murder, as instead of frightening her, it convinced her more. Thus, she continued organizing in the Union, always more poor paid women who were working in inadequate conditions in factories and stores such as the ones belonging to Bufalino and Anastasia. Matheson did so, although even her superiors in the Union, back in New York, warned her repeatedly to be careful and let go. And, of course, despite the continuous threats of the crime family. Until 1953, she had brought sixty more shops into the Union, with 700 workers.

In doing so, Matheson had stood against another intimidating tactic from Bufalino's part, who had his brother-in-law Angelo Sciandra running the Northeastern Pennsylvania Needle Worker's Association: Another puppet union of his. To convince employees to become members of that Union, they would say: "Sign with us, or you'll be sorry." Matheson did not let go and continued her work in Pittston, where suddenly, one night, as she was walking in the street, a man came and told her that the Bufalino's men had told him to close his shop, threatening him that they would harm his family if he didn't.

Again, other than being intimidated, Matheson used this fact to make the situation public, promoting her struggle with interviews to newspapers and radio, saying that "to live by permission of goons is worse than death. Gentlemen, hoodlums, I don't scare easily." Another characteristic similar event happened in 1955. Matheson and members of the Union protested in front of a store that belonged to Bufalino, and his men ironized them, telling them that they should bring their husbands too. Then, Matheson, having seen that Bufalino himself was in front of the shop, went straight to his face and said: "I don't need my husband to protect me. I'm twice the man you'll ever be, Russ Bufalino."

Bufalino's Grasp on the Teamsters Union

Nevertheless, the problems given to him by Matheson's determination did not mean that Bufalino's position in relation to labor unions was that bad. In 1946, Bufalino moved his cousin William Bufalino to Detroit, where the latter was appointed as leader of Detroit Teamsters Local 985, which was controlled by Jimmy Hoffa. This fact gave more opportunities to Bufalino and strengthened his position as he came closer to a rising union leader.

Bufalino became increasingly influential in the Teamsters Union during the late 1940s and early 1950s, and that, by the mid-1950s, earned him 5% of every loan friends and collaborators took thanks to the facilitations he was able to offer. His influence in the Union was due in great part to his cousins William Bufalino and Jimmy Hoffa.

However, in 1953, the U.S. House subcommittee with chairman Representative Clare E. Hoffman was formed. The new subcommittee's mission would be to investigate cases of racketeering in Detroit, following the work of the Kefauver Committee and the interest it had brought to the Mafia issue. Soon, the Hoffman Committee managed to discover what was happening in Hoffa's 985 Detroit local, paying attention to the activity of William Bufalino.

The committee's report mentioned that in Detroit, not only the unorganized workers but also the workers who were members of unions, businessmen who were independent, and even sometimes the Federal Government were victims of a "gigantic, wicked conspiracy," which used to extort and accumulate millions of dollars through force, threats, and economic pressure. The report made it clear that the "principal offender and perpetrator of the racketeering, extortion, and gangsterism" was the Local 985 Teamsters Union through its president, William Bufalino.

However, the committee was proven incapable of practically diminishing the Mafia's grasp on the Union. Having Hoffa on his part, Bufalino continued to control the Teamsters Union efficiently and profitably for him. But a tangible effect came through. The FBI, which had for a long questioned and rejected the very existence of the Mafia, was obliged to accept it. The next step was the beginning of the Top Hoodlum Program, ordered by J. Edgar Hoover. The goal of the project was to document in detail the most powerful leaders of organized crime in the United States and their businesses and operations. Many agents participated, following and taking notice of the Mafia bosses' activities. One of the latter was obviously Russell Bufalino.

Bufalino Keeps Rising

From the beginning of the 1950s, Russell Bufalino was undoubtedly a very powerful boss of the Pittston Mafia. Fundamental to his rise had been the fact that he had the opportunity to have as advisors and mentors gangsters like Santo Volpe and Charles Bufalino, his uncle, and above all, Stefano Magaddino. Years before, the former had a durable impact on the Wyoming Valley, using the typical Mafia instruments of murdering and bribing the right people. For his part, Magaddino was always the leader of the Buffalo crime family, where Russell Bufalino had grown up and began his mobster career.

Bufalino was not active only in the Pittston and Scranton area or in New York. He had interests in Philadelphia, too, where Angelo Bruno, a good friend of his, was a big deal in the organized crime world, as his father was the boss of the Philadelphia Mafia. In 1946, his father died, and Angelo Bruno became the new boss, gaining the nickname of "Gentle Don," as his way of doing business was based more on negotiation, even though he regularly used violence. The point is he was more prompt to act diplomatically than his friend Russ, who was also skillful with working in the background but more prone to conflict and violent resolution of issues.

In 1954, the first FBI report on Bufalino was ready in the Philadelphia Top Hoodlum file. According to the report, by the early to mid-1950s, Russell Bufalino had become one of the two most powerful Mafia leaders in Pittston. He was the active boss of the local crime family, while Santo Vole and his uncle Charles Bufalino acted as silent partners. The report mentioned that Bufalino worked as a mechanic in a bottling factory run by Joseph Barbara during World War II, which was located in Binghamton, New York. But by the time of the report, Bufalino reportedly had seven dress factories in the area of Pittston. Also, he controlled the gambling activities in the area, as everybody who was involved in them had to pay him a "cut."

In 1953, Bufalino reportedly controlled around twenty of the dress factories existing in Pittston, directly or through members of the family. Moreover, to enter the garment industry in the region, someone had to come to an agreement with Bufalino, who earned money from the clothes manufactured by producers who had a contract with him. Apart from what is mentioned in the FBI report, we know that Bufalino also owned banks, jewelry shops, hotels, and restaurants. The report talked about Bufalino's contacts and collaborations with other gangsters, like Angelo Bruno. The agents followed him and registered everything. On his trips to New York every week, he stayed more often at the Hotel Forrester and a few times at the Hotel New Yorker and the Hotel Lexington. In Pittston, Bufalino often visited the Imperial Poolroom, while in Scranton, he had an office near the Martz bus terminal.

Also, the report mentioned that Bufalino controlled all gambling in the area. If you wanted to bet on baseball, football, or basketball games, you earned him money. His best friend was William Medico, who was a businessman and owned the Medico Electric Company. But he had also passed from illegal businesses during Prohibition, operating in the bootlegging sector before turning to be a respectable entrepreneur and respectful toward the law. That explains his close friendship with Bufalino and the fact that Medico was considered a leader in the inner circles of the Northeastern Pennsylvania crime family, which we can now begin to call the Bufalino crime family. There were also suspicions that the real owner of Medico Electric Company was Bufalino himself and that Medico was a facade.

Every Wednesday, Bufalino usually returned to Scranton from New York and had dinner with his wife Carolyn and friends, often in some of his own restaurants. He typically enjoyed red wine, pasta, and chicken or fish. He was also a good cook, as he liked and relaxed by cooking sometimes and eating with friends and collaborators, talking about fun things or business. In New York, he used to go on Monday mornings taking flights from an airport near Scranton, the airport of Avoca, Pennsylvania. Bufalino was also competent with what mattered most, that is, the politicians and the police. He was very attentive to their needs and desires to keep them happy with their lives in the way that was more suitable in every case, from doing favors to passing them money.

Another important characteristic of Russell Bufalino was his friendly attitude toward people who had nothing to do with his criminal activities and businesses. He was kind and respectful, and not surprisingly, he was often seen in a positive way. A telling anecdote they say about this aspect of Bufalino was when one day he saw a man doing work on the roof of his house. It was a scorching summer day, and it was noon, so he told his men to go to the roof and do the work for the man, saving him from the scorching sun.

In 1956, Bufalino, accompanied by his second in command, James Osticco and Medico, traveled to Cuba and stayed there for a month in Havana amidst casinos and dazzling nightclubs. That wasn't his first trip to Cuba, but it was the first that the FBI was watching him. On that occasion to Cuba, Bufalino met Santo Trafficante Jr., with whom he was co-owner of a nightclub called Sans Souci. Trafficante was the boss of the South Florida crime family.

CHAPTER 4
CRIMINAL ENTERPRISES TAKE SHAPE

This chapter examines the Mafia's massive investment in Cuba during the years of Fulgencio Batista, whose policy was to attract investment from solid economic actors from the United States without distinctions between legal and illegal. We will see how it all began after a summit legendary gangster Lucky Luciano called in Havana in 1946 to discuss and organize the entrance of heroin to the American market and how Russell Bufalino was one of the bosses who collaborated closer with Batista, gaining money, while excelled in criminal activities back home, such as loan-sharking and infiltrating labor unions. The Bufalino crime family also had legitimate businesses, but violence and intimidation were essential; that's why the chapter closes by introducing a characteristic gangster, Frank Sheeran.

Cuba Business

By the time the Second World War started, Lucky Luciano was convicted for pandering and put in jail. Though the emergency condition of those bloody days for the world was a bit of great luck for him, the validation of his name, as the need for the American government to control the East Coast docks and also the waterfronts, preventing German agents from causing sabotage, gave Luciano a precious opportunity. He came to an agreement with the authorities, according to which he positioned his men in the area as counter-espionage and counter-sabotage in service of the government. In this way, when the war was over victoriously for the Allies, the New York governor, Thomas E. Dewey, gave Luciano a pardon as a reward for his help.

However, the deal was on under the condition that Luciano would leave the United States. Indeed, he went to Italy and found a way to make his permanence there promising from an organized crime point of view. In Italy, he learned about and understood how profitable the new drug named heroin could be. So, he called for a meeting of all the Mafia families' bosses in Cuba, who gathered in a meeting that had historic proportions for organized crime. Names of powerful Mafia bosses we have seen, like Stefano Magaddino, Frank Costello, and Albert Anastasia, participated in the Havana meeting in 1946. There, Lucky Luciano explained what a great opportunity and immense potential introducing heroin in a huge, new market like the one of the United States would have, and they talked of how the drug flows from Italy to the United States could be organized.

In the background, but rising and growing in status, Russell Bufalino was present at the 1946 Italian-American Mafia summit of Havana, as Magaddino had his lieutenants from Buffalo and Scranton coming with him in Cuba. Bufalino was not a factor in this meeting, which decided the heroin to come to Cuba first and then be transported to the United States. Not a factor, but growing, and also in his first trip to a country that will occupy a crucial role in his future operations as a Mafia boss.

Beginning in the late 1940s and then much more during the 1950s, Bufalino was a close friend of the Cuban dictator and president,

Fulgencio Batista. In power essentially from 1933, after a revolt through controlled presidents, the former military sergeant became officially president of Cuba in 1940, winning the elections.

The US government had recognized the new Cuban governments controlled by Batista from 1934, as he was very attentive to securing the favor of the Americans. Not only the politicians and diplomats. Also, the gangsters. During his years as the leader of Cuba, Batista collaborated tightly with organized crime based in the United States, buying and building hotels and casinos on the island, which was becoming a resort for American and European tourists, almost something like a Las Vegas in the middle of the sea, developed in parallel with the actual Las Vegas.

Batista expanded and grew his business even more after he lost the elections of 1944—which was kind of strange and maybe shows that, at that point, he was sincere about wanting to make Cuba a democratic country. Anyway, Batista made the most of his year out of the presidency by often visiting his houses in Florida and New York and mostly making friends.

Obviously, democracy soon became very boring to Batista, who in 1952 preferred to return to power with a coup instead of elections. President Dwight Eisenhower recognized the new Cuban government, which maybe wasn't democratic but was certainly friendly to the United States and American investment. Indeed, Batista quickly stipulated agreements with many American companies, and with the sector of the economy, he knew even better that of organized crime. The Cuban Las Vegas project gained new momentum as Batista made anything he could to attire investments in hotels and casinos. And he did it. In the next years, almost all big Mafia bosses in the United States invested in Cuban hotels and casinos, like Sans Souci, Plaza, Sevilla-Biltmore, Nacional, and

Commodoro. The mastermind of the US crime families' contacts and agreements with Batista was always Lucky Luciano. Their coordinator and representative was one of his close collaborators, the Jewish mobster Meyer Lansky.

We must say that the project seemed to work well. Those choices brought huge amounts of money to Cuba, with many American rich seeing it as a good opportunity to invest. The Cuban economy grew, and some Cubans began to create considerable wealth. First of all, Batista himself got bribes from construction companies that wanted to get deals for work in the country, like highways and airports. Plus, Batista had 10-30% of the casinos' revenues, which offered earnings of more than one million dollars per day to the crime families in the USA. It was a win-win situation, wonderful also for Russell Bufalino.

Bufalino was not just one of the gangsters who did business with Batista in Cuba. He was also a really close friend of the corrupted Cuban president. It's telling that Batista's kids used to take vacations in Northeastern Pennsylvania, guarded and protected by Bufalino.

So, by 1956, Russell Bufalino had amassed a large fortune from his control of the wealth on the island of Cuba, his influence in the Teamsters Union, particularly its Central States pension funds, as well as from his grasp over the garment industry, and numerous other companies in Pennsylvania and New York. Bufalino was also involved in a number of other businesses in both of these states. After John Sciandra died and Bufalino took over as the head of the family in Northeastern Pennsylvania in 1949, he was also recognized as one of the most important Mafia bosses in the United States. Meanwhile, Joseph Barbara still held the reins of the southern tier of New York despite having suffered two heart attacks within one calendar year and being in bad health.

So, by the time he reached his mid-fifties, Bufalino had earned the respect of his peers in the criminal underworld as one of the most powerful criminals in the nation. Nevertheless, very few people outside of organized crime circles knew or heard of him, and those who did have a difficult time comprehending how a crime boss from Northeastern Pennsylvania could wield more authority than a crime leader from New York or Chicago. But this is exactly what he managed to do.

A series of criminal activities executed with precision and efficiency by his crime family, which followed the lead and the example of its quiet, cool, and not cocky boss, brought Bufalino to that elevated position among American organized crime. The most important of them are examined in the following paragraphs.

Loan-Sharking

One of the criminal enterprises the Bufalino crime family was definitely involved with was loan-sharking, which means that they provided loans at very high, usurious text rates. The usual rate they asked for was 20% per week, thus around a 1000% annual rate. Although the terms of the repayment could vary and consist of sometimes unorthodox arrangements, there is no doubt that this kind of rate was illegal and violated Pennsylvania's laws on loans, a criminal act.

Loan sharks were attracted by desperate people who couldn't provide collateral to obtain a loan from a bank in a legitimate way. Those borrowers had often defaulted and failed to cover earlier debts. They were eager to find a way to get cash quickly, putting themselves in an extremely precarious and dangerous situation, as the Mafia loan sharks didn't hesitate to collect debts in a forceful manner, creating fear and using intimidation, a very useful atmosphere to them. There were many examples of assaults or at least threats against borrowers.

On the other side, sometimes borrowers would resort to loan sharks out of an unfair inability to have access to legitimate loans because they were erroneously characterized as "high risk." Loan sharks, in those cases, appeared as a way out of the deadlock. The problem is that, more often, they proved to be a far worse and more dangerous deadlock than a way out of it.

There were loan sharks and their associates who ended up arrested and convicted after legal recourses by borrowers. However, the Bufalino family was not one of them.

Infiltration Into Labor Unions

It was typical routine for families implicated in organized crime to try to establish friends and relatives of theirs in roles of authority inside labor unions. This way, they had the opportunity to exert leverage and supervision over the functions and finances of the labor unions. To force union the leaders and the members of unions into conceding to the directives of the criminal organizations, the criminal syndicates employed a combination of actions, including menaces and intimidation. In case the union officials stood up to those demands, they could enter at risk of being attacked physically.

Operations of racketeering were carried out by Mafia families using labor unions as their instruments. That kind of operation could be a variety of unlawful things in any precise case, such as loansharking, appropriation of union money, and illegal gambling, to name just a few.

The effects labor union infiltration by crime families like the Bufalino one had on labor relations, particular industries, and local economies were wide and heavily influenced local societies, business, and their everyday lives and work.

The infiltration of unions often created good examples of corruption, of course, and also of nepotism inside these institutions. All of that had the unsurprising effect of influencing labor relations in a deeply negative way. Corporations linked in one way or another to organized crime often profited from union contracts, which resulted in treating employees not in a just way. It's obvious that often, the workers' rights and interests, like salaries, job security, and safety in work, were at risk when union officials were more focused on helping criminal organizations profit and expand their influence and reach than on the needs and desires of the unions' members. The Bufalino crime family and other Mafia families often orchestrated strikes, stoppages, or slowdowns of the productions not to promote the interests of the employees but to make employers concede to the family's demands and extortion.

The Bufalino crime family tried to gain economic power over lawful companies by controlling labor unions, using them as leverage instruments. Influence over unions meant influence on legitimate businesses as well, by implication. In order to obtain a direct and easy way to the treasuries of the unions, funds for pensions. It was also a method to extort businessmen, as mentioned, and at the same time to get workers to spend money on gambling or get loans with the huge loan shark interest rates we've seen.

The goal to control labor unions, in the beginning, was achieved mostly by using brutal violence, such as killings and destroying facilities. Over time, the Mafia's operating mode on this issue went from raw violence to a more businesslike, indirect approach, with the use of strikes and slowdowns from the workers or by just threatening the employers that they would have the workers doing them. Of course, violence was not abandoned altogether—intimidation and coercion were always in the game.

Another tactic was the so-called "sweetheart contracts." Union officials were given money illegally to keep the workplace in peace from the labor point of view, keeping the workers calm.

A lot of people who were involved in racketeering of this kind, between labor leaders and management, met prosecution by the federal government, and some were sentenced. With those prosecutions, the state aimed to stop the criminal operations of corruption in the internal labor unions, whose reason for existing should be the protection and promotion of the employees' rights and interests.

The entry of organized crime in labor unions and companies provoked greater costs for the industries impacted by it, as the corrupt practices diminished efficiency and damaged the function of those industries. That was bad news for companies and consumers alike, as it meant lower profits for the former and higher expenses for the latter.

It was also sometimes feasible for criminal organizations to corrupt competition in sectors of the economy where they had control over labor unions or companies by favoring economic actors with whom they collaborated at the expense of others. Moreover, unions and enterprises under organized crime are certainly more prone to illegal and unethical acts themselves, such as exploiting the employees, acting like cartels that fix prices, and manipulating bids for public works.

All those practices probably resulted in the loss of jobs for people. Although this is not a measurable effect, we can consider that organized crime corruption damaged companies or forced them to relocate to other regions, with employment losses. Moreover, the crime families influence over companies, markets, and labor unions comprehensibly canceled or made much more difficult and discouraged companies and corporations that had plans of investing in certain areas and local industries.

And the negative consequences were not strictly economic but also social. Corrupted labor unions with criminal presence, influence, or total control profoundly damaged communities that now lived in an atmosphere of intimidation, fear, and lack of trust. Fascinating as they may seem to many people, those mobsters provoked great problems in human relationships and the cohesion and joy of everyday life of local communities under their violent and bullying supervision or control.

Members of criminal organizations can infiltrate legitimate businesses for various reasons. At times, they could do it to obtain a source of income that will function as a cover for their true criminal professional activities, as well as facilitate money laundering operations.

The appropriation of legal companies by criminal organizations can happen through many different strategies: violence, threats, and seizure of debt to grab the rate of a company. Over time, the criminal organizations expand their grasp and operate in order to impose their monopoly on the sector they put under pressure, expelling in one way or another all the previous actors.

When that finally happened, the criminal organization could use its political connections and alliances to gain protection and tax breaks. Don't forget the cheap and quiet labor power thanks to the crime family's leverage or control on labor unions. Illegal operations in legitimate businesses typically followed, including evading taxes, cheating insurance companies, and false bankrupting, in a chain of lawless and criminal actions.

A very simple example could be that money gained from debts on gambling was an excellent capital for loan-sharking operations. Another example could be that declaring false bankruptcy defrauded creditors, and then assets were hidden and sold in the black market illegally.

Criminal organization members could be owners or co-owners of numerous and very different, and as we've already seen, the Bufalino crime family had its hands on hotels, casinos, the garment industry, restaurants, construction companies, and more.

Extortion

Crime families like the Bufalino one sold so-called protection to businesses, pretending that they would keep their clients safe from possible danger. To do this, they must be paid on a constant basis, of course. And that's where the trick is: if they don't get paid, they will cause themselves the damage they expect to be paid to prevent. It is a genius scheme, as, in fact, they aren't even lying: They indeed protect their "clients" from being harmed by themselves. The same genius strategy could be used in a slightly different way, by demanding money or a profitable attitude and management to offer favorable treatment or take care of issues that the crime family had created or fomented in the first place.

Another method was contacting the owners of companies or properties and demanding that they accept members of the crime family as partners, threatening to use violence or disturb the function of the company if the owner refused. The violence and the threats were headed not only toward the counterpart of the negotiation but also their families, including their children, according to the most noble Mafia traditions. The same peaceful arguments were used to convince owners to sell their properties at lower prices than the actual ones.

Another method to extort people was acquiring sensitive information and then threatening that they would expose uncomfortable or embarrassing facts if the poor victims didn't concede to the demands of the Mafia boss.

Intimidation, blackmail, violence, and threats all aimed to foment fear and panic in order for the victims to succumb psychologically and become subdued subjects to the will of the crime family. On the other hand, the most typical way to deal with politicians and law enforcement in order to avoid their reaction to extortion was to bribe and affect them with any means necessary.

A Characteristic Gangster: The "Irishman"

One could ask oneself what kind of people could be capable of conducting those kinds of activities and actions in a profitable way without remorse. One of the best examples of the essential gangster of that time, who made possible all of the above at the operational everyday level, on the streets of the cities and the towns where the Mafia families put their tentacles, was definitely Frank Sheeran.

During the mid-1900s, when Russell Bufalino was rising to become a powerful Mafia boss in Northeastern Pennsylvania and at the national level, a key figure in the organized crime universe was Frank Sheeran, born Francis Joseph Sheeran in 1920. Known as the "Irishman," Sheeran and his criminal career were connected to Bufalino and thus with the Mafia.

Before that, Sheeran had served in the Army during World War II, where he took part in the Italian Campaign and had the experience of heavy combat. Apart from that, he participated in less honorable situations and, to be more precise, in executions of German prisoners of war, which, of course, violated the Geneva Convention.

All this should not be considered an excuse or explanation for the occupation Sheeran would choose to follow, though. Not only because millions of people have fought in bloody wars, which sometimes crossed the boundaries of international war law, without becoming criminals afterward. But also because Sheeran entered the world of organized crime ten years after the end of the war. It all started in 1955, when "The Irishman" met Russell Bufalino. Sheeran's truck, while he was working as a driver for a food company, was broken, and Bufalino, being the nice guy we saw he was in his non-gangster life, offered to get it fixed. In this case, the new friendship would evolve into doing some business together, first, with Sheeran being Bufalino's driver and delivery boy. Then, with less peaceful activities.

It seems that at the beginning, he started working for organized crime as a bully who intimidated people and smashed things. That's how he was hired by Whispers DiTullio, a mobster who needed somebody to smash the Cadillac Linen Service in Delaware for good and was willing to pay $10,000 for that. Sheeran tried to do the job, but he didn't know that Cadillac Linen Service's owner was Angelo Bruno. The latter's men caught Sheeran before he accomplished his mission and brought him to their boss. And he would be about to have the most serious trouble if it wasn't for Bufalino, who learned what happened and intervened to save him. They made a deal, though. Sheeran had to kill DiTullio. And so he did. As said in his autobiography, this was the first Mafia murder Sheeran committed.

Later, now a full associate of the crime family, Bualino introduced Sheeran to Jimmy Hoffa, the labor union leader of Teamsters International. Also, Hoffa thought that "The Irishman" could be a good friend and mostly a valuable option for carrying out a series of tough missions of intimidation and killing of union members who weren't loyal to him or killing members of competitor unions. Apparently, over time, Hoffa thought that Sheeran was good for other jobs, too, and he appointed him as acting president of Local 326 in Wilmington, Delaware, one of the departments of the Teamsters Union.

Sheeran would be imprisoned in October 1980, convicted for eleven cases of labor racketeering. The sentence was 32 years in jail, and he served 13. Before that, he had been accused or suspected of several murders, like the ones of Robert DeGeorge in 1967, Joe Gallo in 1972, Francis J. Marino in 1976, and Frederick John Gawronski again in 1976.

"The Irishman" died on December 14, 2003, at 83, nine years after the death of Russell Bufalino, his mentor and boss, who introduced him to organized crime half a century before. However, the most crucial chapter in the criminal career of Frank Sheeran was maybe one we haven't talked about yet. That's his role in the murder of Jimmy Hoffa.

CHAPTER 5
LAW ENFORCEMENT'S INVOLVEMENT

This chapter brings us to the biggest gathering of crime bosses in United States history, made in Apalachin in 1957. The arch-gangsters discussed business and the Lucky Luciano family succession. Russell Bufalino was there, and he was one of the bosses who got arrested after the surprise police operation. The event proved the existence of the Mafia and prompted law enforcement to use more sophisticated methods to battle organized crime, such as new technologies of surveillance and witness protection programs. After Apalachin, the FBI paid much more attention to the Bufalino crime family. Bufalino had severe problems with the law, as he was ordered to leave the U.S.

Becoming Nationwide Famous in the Wrong Way: The Apalachin Meeting

On November 14, 1957, Russell Bufalino was at 625 McFall Road in Apalachin, New York. He was anything but alone. Around a hundred other high-ranking gangsters were at the same place for what would go down in history as the Apalachin Meeting, the greatest gathering of the Italian-American Mafia bosses. The place was the house of Joseph Barbara, and the topics of discussion were loan-sharking, trafficking of drugs, illegal gambling, and other

Mafia businesses, as well as splitting the activities of Albert Anastasia, who had been murdered a few time ago.

The meeting was at Barbara's residence in Apalachin, but the one who had called that nationwide organized crime conference was Vito Genovese. Genovese's goal was also to make official his assuming the leadership of the Lucky Luciano family after Frank Costello's forced backdown.

Origins of the Apalachin Meeting

That last phrase would need a more detailed explanation. Not only because the particularities of the Apalachin Meeting are interesting per se, but also, and most importantly, because they give us the opportunity to delve deeper into the secrets and mysteries of organized crime in the 20th century United States.

Indeed, this story goes back more than twenty years and includes some of the most famous (or infamous) Italian-American Mafiosi.

It was June 18, 1936, when legendary Mafia boss Lucky Luciano and others were convicted to the devastating sentence of 30-50 years in prison. Almost ten years later, on January 3, 1946, New York state governor Thomas E. Dewey grudgingly mitigated Luciano's sentence on the condition that he not oppose being deported to Italy. This mitigation was a putative reward for Luciano's purported wartime aid to the United States (we'll talk more about that later). Luciano happily took the offer but insisted that he was a citizen of the United States, thus not liable to be deported to Italy or another country. Nevertheless, he had to depart with a ship from the port of Brooklyn on February 10, 1946. That day was the last he ever stood on U.S. soil. After seventeen days, Luciano's ship entered the port of Naples. It was February 28, and he informed the journalists who awaited him upon his arrival that he would most likely live in Sicily.

The next year, 1937, the acting boss of the Luciano crime family, Vito Genovese, after the murder of Ferdinand Boccia and concerned about the possibility of being prosecuted, had to leave the U.S. too, and he went to Italy, taking with him $750,000. He would settle in Nola, near Naples, the hometown of the famous philosopher Giordano Bruno, who was burnt alive for heresy by the Sacred Inquisition of the Catholic Church back in 1600.

The problem was that after Genovese left the States, the Luciano family needed a new acting boss. That would be Frank Costello. The scheme functioned well for some years, but in the mid-1950s, Genovese felt it was time to take back control of the family. His ambition was so big, and perhaps his memory for the reason of Costello's rise so short, that he was determined to hit even against the very powerful ally on which Costello could count: The leader of the Anastasia crime family and firm member of the Commission, Albert Anastasia.

Luckily enough, his intentions found an unlikely ally, as Genovese managed to find a link and join forces with the underboss of the Anastasia crime family, Carlo Gambino. Seeking to become the top dog, Gambino met his opportunity in Genovese's intentions, and they both began planning to take Anastasia out for good. It must be noted, though, that apart from Gambino's goals, according to a theory, Anastasia's violent ways of acting had become frustrating not only for Gambino but also for many Commission members, who sanctioned or gave permission for his assassination, believing that it would be in Mafia's best interest as a whole.

At the beginning of 1957, Genovese felt the pieces were in place to make his move in collaboration with Gambino. He ordered a hitman named Vincent Gigante to kill Costello, and Gigante shot him on May 2, 1957, outside the building where Costello lived.

Costello was not killed, and his wound was also not so serious. Nevertheless, this attack, and maybe the swift power he felt that happened, made him think that it would be better if he retired and gave back control of the Luciano family to Genovese. The fact that he wanted to stay out of trouble and that the whole balance of power inside the Mafia world was not in his favor can also be deducted from his refusing to recognize Gigante as the gunman who had shot him when the latter was put on trial. Thanks to Costello's omission, Gigante was free of charges.

Of course, that happened after the conclusion of the Anastasia removal, which was consumed on October 25, 1957. That day, Genovese and Gambino's plan was executed in perfection, as two gunmen with covered faces shot Anastasia to death in the Park Central Hotel barber shop in Manhattan. Genovese had heard that Costello was plotting with Anastasia to regain the Luciano crime family's leadership.

That was the long sequence of Mafia events that led to the infamous Apalachin Meeting, a focal point of organized crime's history in the United States. A few days after Anastasia's murder, seeking legitimation and wanting to secure and stabilize his grasp of the Luciano family, Genovese organized that big meeting, which was also an opportunity for American Cosa Nostra bosses to arrange a series of business staff. The initial idea was that the meeting be held in Chicago. Still, Stefano Magaddino, the powerful New York boss who was also a Commission member and the mentor of Russell Bufalino, insisted the meeting be held nearer to his base and appointed Joseph Barbara and Russell Bufalino to take care of everything. Barbara's estate in Apalachin, New York, along the southern side of the Susquehanna River, should be the perfect place, but it wasn't.

The Apalachin Meeting Fiasco and Its Consequences

On November 14, 1957, over 100 Mafia leaders, advisors, and bodyguards gathered at Barbara's estate in Apalachin. The meeting's goal was, as already explained, double. On the one hand, to discuss regular Cosa Nostra business, thus activities like illegal gambling, casinos, and narcotics deals. There were also garment industry discussions, particularly interesting for Russell Bufalino, as we can imagine.

On the other hand, the second goal was the division of criminal enterprises headed until then by Albert Anastasia, who was just assassinated. Before the Commission authorized his assassination, powerful family bosses and, among them, Bufalino, were concerned about Anastasia's attempts to wrest control of their Havana casino operations. Cuba was also discussed in Apalachin, specifically the island's gambling and drug smuggling activities.

Another essential item on the agenda was the worldwide drug trade. Recently, just before the meeting in Apalachin, some Italian-American Cosa Nostra leaders had visited Palermo, where they met with Sicilian gangsters to talk about the trafficking routes and methods.

Unluckily for the elite of organized crime, law enforcement had come to know about the meeting and the great opportunity to arrest and put charges on such a large number of Mafia bosses. The numerous luxury automobiles with license plates from all over the United States gathered in a quiet Apalachin residence did not help the mob leaders keep the eyes of the police away from them. State and local agency officials stormed the Barbara estate after erecting barricades to the streets in order to cut the way out of the area. With nothing else to do, many bosses ran and tried to hide in the surrounding woods.

Some managed to escape, but the majority, some sixty gangsters, including Russell Bufalino and his underboss James Osticco, were arrested and charged. Twenty of the participants at the gathering were put on trial and found guilty of "conspiring to obstruct justice by lying about the nature of the underworld meeting." They were convicted to three to five years in jail, plus fines of up to $10,000. However, one year later, all the sentences were overthrown in the appeal court.

Even more important than the arrests of so many top organized crime figures was the mere fact of the confirmation that the Mafia existed, that it was not a conspiracy theory but a real criminal organization at the national level, or better, a net of numerous interconnected criminal organizations. That was really crucial, as until the Apalachin meeting, even the director of the FBI, Edgar Hoover, had repeatedly rejected the notion that such a thing existed in the United States, at least officially.

The Bufalino Crime Family Targeted by Law Enforcement

As an immediate reaction to the growing power and involvement of the Bufalino crime family in an extensive range of illegal operations, the authorities got more active in their inquiries and efforts to tear down the criminal organization.

The fruit of this new tendency in law enforcement's acts was that authorities undertook several legal procedures against the crime family's structure.

Particularly from 1957, following the notorious Apalachin meeting that we covered in detail above, the Bufalino crime family became known to the public. The meeting and the intervention of the police were undoubtedly critical points in the evolution of the government's efforts to counter organized crime as law enforcement agents intervened, arresting many bosses. Some of them managed to escape prosecution and charges by making appeals. Nevertheless, this incursion revealed the volume of organized crime and prompted law enforcement to take even more intense action against it as public awareness elevated.

The authorities understood that they had to pay more attention to the Bufalino family, too. Then, they recruited people who could give information on that crime family. Some of those informants came from within the family and became witnesses under police protection. The witnesses gave very useful insights into the organization's system, operations, and leaders.

The law enforcement agents investigated the criminal activities of various Mafia families, including the Bufalino crime family, conducting surveillance, using wiretaps and other methods to collect proof against the organization's components and associates. They aimed to hurt the Bufalino crime family's finances, the point it would hurt the most, and they employed measures to seize the earnings of criminal operations, undermining the family's economic foundations. The authorities utilized financial documents, inspections, and accounting investigations in order to successfully trace the money movements and confiscate patrimonial assets when they had the chance.

Coordinating their efforts, law enforcement was able to comprehend deeply how the Bufalino crime family functioned and, above all, that its activities were not limited to Northeastern

Pennsylvania but were nationwide. They also pursued collaboration with various communities that had contact with the family's activities in their local reality to put it smoothly. The local communities indeed often collaborated since the Bufalino effect on them was not the best thing that ever happened to them.

Local communities' cooperation and coordination among the authorities themselves gave fruits, as cases against gangsters were built based on the information gathered.

Techniques to Combat Organized Crime

The techniques used to combat organized crime with greater efficiency were multiple, like the creation of task forces, the use of new technologies, new surveillance methods, witness protection, and collaboration among law enforcement agencies we've already seen.

The task forces were specialized teams that enabled cooperative operations by bringing together the expertise and resources of authorities of different levels, from local to federal. The use of new technological advances like electronic spying and wiretapping made surveillance much more sophisticated and precise, and collecting evidence and clues much more feasible for monitoring suspects and getting to know Mafia family members' moves and plans. When this kind of technology wasn't available, the ability of law enforcement to penetrate criminal organizations was much smaller.

The witness protection programs also played a crucial role in X-ray criminal organizations and put their members behind bars. They encouraged witnesses to talk to the police and kept safe those who did, giving incentives also to members of crime families. Another method law enforcement used to get into Mafia structures and minds was covert informants. They weren't members of the organizations who decided to collaborate with the authorities but agents of law enforcement agencies who infiltrated criminal organizations, offering direct information from within.

All of the above could work better and give positive results if the general public was aware and willing to help law enforcement's efforts to counter organized crime. So, the operational techniques accompanied public awareness projects, with which the authorities encouraged and motivated people to report when they happened to see something suspicious that could be part of a criminal activity. Educating the communities about the Mafia and organized crime, the authorities also hoped to have more people willing to work with the police as informants and undercover agents.

The pressure applied by the authorities, thanks to those techniques, methods, and means, created a much less comfortable situation for organized crime and made the continuation of illegal activities, like the ones of the Bufalino crime family, harder.

Informants and Witnesses

The role of informants and witnesses was crucial in helping law enforcement face the Mafia challenge, as they offered precious inside information on the criminal organizations. Their contributions, which offered knowledge of the operations and internal structure otherwise not accessible, allowed the authorities to raise more solid and founded cases against members and leaders of criminal organizations like the Bufalino crime family.

Doing so was not easy for informants and witnesses since they could endure serious physical dangers and suffer stress and emotional pressure because of their choice to cooperate with the police. Cooperating could expose them or people close to them to retaliation. Informants often lived in a constant sense of threat and risk, fearing they could be discovered and under mental strain because of the continuous secrecy and pretending. On the other hand, witness protection programs were created to respond to the reality of danger and fear faced by witnesses, securing the lives and identities of people who choose to help the police. However, on the other hand, entering such a program could mean cutting oneself off friends and relatives and abandoning one's personal life altogether to begin a new, and at least initially lonely, path. To add to that, in some cases, informants and witnesses did not experience only external threat and danger but also internal struggle, remorse, hesitation, and a sense of guilt because of their decision to cooperate with law enforcement against what until then was their family, friends, and partners.

Nevertheless, there were many valid reasons for a crime family member to become an informant or witness and cooperate with law enforcement. Leaving behind the mobster's way of life and protecting their community from activities they had come to consider damaging and harmful, retaliating for wrongdoings against them, or seeking protection from an already existent threat to their life or those of their loved ones were some of the most important.

And often, their decision was a successful one. It wasn't easy, but the help offered by informants and witnesses was crucial for law enforcement agents to proceed with their investigations and deal with organized crime, dismantling Mafia families by bringing them to the court of law and convicting their leaders and members to be enclosed in jail or reducing the criminal organizations' reach and strength. The programs resulted in success in many cases and helped law enforcement, putting the Bufalino crime family in serious trouble.

Federal Bureau of Investigations Vs. Russell Bufalino

In 1958, after the Apalachin meeting and the arrest the previous year, Bufalino was ordered to leave the United States because he had lied about his citizenship, he had entered the country illegally in 1956 from the Bahamas, and his moral character did not appear to be that good. From that point and for several years on, avoiding deportation became one of the biggest concerns Bufalino had. That's why he hired a lawyer who was a known expert in immigration issues, Jack Wasserman. Wasserman had already managed with success a similar case, that of New Orleans Mafia boss Carlos Marcello. The latter was ordered to leave the country in 1952, initially in Italy. Wasserman delayed the deportation, getting from the Italian courts an injunction that prevented Marcello from going to Italy as he was not an Italian citizen. So, in 1959, they sent Marcello to Guatemala, but Wasserman found a way to make him return to New Orleans.

Bufalino hoped that Wasserman would save him from being deported, too. His case was also easier since it was determined that the whole issue came from a change in Bufalino's place of birth, made by someone in the Luzerne County Clerk Office, who had replaced "Montedoro, Sicily" with "Pittston, Pa." After a series decisions and appeals beginning in April 1958, two years later the U.S. Court of Appeals ordered Bufalino to leave the country, in April 1960. Bufalino and his lawyer filed one more appeal and accused the U.S. Immigration and Naturalization Service of having prejudiced him. That move gave him some time so he could stay in the country until a decision was taken on his appeal.

Since 1961, the new attorney general of the FBI was Robert F. Kennedy, who aimed to destroy organized crime. And he was the brother of the President of the United States, which made things even more complicated for the Mafia bosses. Kennedy did not want to waste any more time. He ordered the FBI agents to surveil every move of the Mafia bosses, each and every one of them, each and every day. Obviously, Bufalino was one of them.

The FBI agents began surveilling Bufalino on a 24-hour basis in March 1961, and the reports arrived at J. Edgar Hoover from the Philadelphia bureau every Monday, Wednesday, and Friday. They soon had the information according to which Bufalino was sending to Cuba arms. The interesting part is that the informant claimed that Bufalino was collaborating with a secret organization. That secret organization was producing arms and passing them to Cuba. The goal was naturally overthrowing Castro. And the irony is that the "secret organization" the FBI didn't know about was simply the CIA. Or maybe that wasn't the case, and in fact, the FBI played ignorant, as their decision not to investigate further on the information may suggest. In any case, the FBI claimed that the issue was out of its jurisdiction. Instead, according to the FBI's decision, the matter was under the Department of Customs' jurisdiction.

However, the FBI kept surveilling Bufalino's activities and contacts. In Pittston, he used to go often to Club 82. In Scranton, he used to go to Preno's Restaurant, to the Sahara Bar, and to the former Medico Electric Company we have seen earlier, which now was called Medico Industries, and had successfully established a collaboration with the U.S. government, firming several contracts. When in New York, Bufalino used to stay in the Forrester Hotel and visit his Vesuvio restaurant, hanging out with notorious New York mobsters. The FBI agents were a little bit surprised to see that New York gangsters had great respect for Bufalino, something that pointed out his national and not just local status as Mafia boss.

In his travels, Bufalino usually had with him some of his closest associates from Northeastern Pennsylvania, like Anthony Guarnieri, who worked as capo regime in the drug traffic sector of the criminal organization; Casper Giumento, who was like the adjutant of the boss, from driver to payments collector; Al Baldassari, the director of the gambling sector; James Plumeri, who was close to Bufalino and had a brilliant Mafia resume as he had worked for Lucky Luciano himself back in the 1930s.

Women and Sports

Probably, most readers will find more exciting Bufalino's relationships with attractive women, as he had many girlfriends in various cities while being happily married to his wife, Carrie, since 1928. In the early 1960s, this men's dream (let's be honest here) had taken the likes of Jane Collins, a rich divorced woman whose housemate was a prostitute named Judy McCarthy. Bufalino used to meet Collins in McCarthy's apartment when McCarthy was not in the city.

To tell the truth, at least in this particular case, Bufalino's motives and attraction to Collins were not only romantic. In fact, it was also his difficult financial state that brought him close to the wealthy divorcee after the disaster in Cuba and the continuous need to spend money on attorneys for the matter of his attempted deportation to Italy. Although definitely not poor or broke, Bufalino could use some of the financial prosperity Collins enjoyed as co-owner of the Wyoming Coal Company. Indeed, Collins obviously really liked Bufalino, and she began to pay his bills and bought him a Cadillac as a birthday present. Or she did so because, for her part, she could use some of Bufalino's muscle to spy on her ex-husband as truly happened.

In 1963, Bufalino and Collins separated, and she started a new relationship with another man. Bufalino was mad and tried to win her back, visiting her several times and yelling at her, but to no avail. The last time he visited her, he talked to her about his deportation battle, and he offered her a New York Yankees-St. Louis Cardinals World Series ticket. Yet, she refused to come with him to New York. Things were way worse than Bufalino could think, as, in fact, Collins had begun to talk to the FBI, which obviously approached her because of her relationship with Bufalino and convinced her to help the immigration department and the law to get the job—that is, to deport Bufalino from the U.S.—done.

However, it could be entertaining to mention the initial approach of Bufalino to Collins. He had a friend call Collins to give her a tip on a horse race, thanks to which Collins bet and won $100. One week later, they gave her another tip, and she won $250. Then, $1000. At this point, Bufalino had to give her the money himself because that was what they used to do in gambling when the earnings were that big.

Sports and gambling were central to Bufalino's entertainment and activities, and he liked boxing particularly, as the FBI agents came to know. During that period, Bufalino also tried to get into the boxing industry by managing boxers and promoting fights. In those activities, Bufalino collaborated with Al Flora, who was a former boxer from Baltimore and also was his occasional bodyguard and driver. Undoubtedly, the most impressive involvement of Bufalino with the boxing and sports industry would come a few years later, in 1965, when he purchased the rights to the closed-circuit broadcast of the second heavyweight championship fight between Cassius Clay (later Mohammed Ali) and Sonny Liston for Washington, D.C.

Bufalino had a wide business circle, yet he kept almost everything in cash and had only a tiny checking account with a few hundred dollars in common with his wife. Maybe this helps to explain how, although he faced financial difficulties, that was never evident when he left Pittston and Scranton and traveled to big cities. The FBI agents noted that when he was in Philadelphia, he used to go out at the Penn Center Social Club with friends. There, he met luxury escorts he paid $600-800 cash each, provided by the choreographer Kay Carlton. He also had another girlfriend in parallel with Collins. Her name was Alberta Stocker, and she was a bartender.

CHAPTER 6

THE TENACITY AND ADAPTABILITY OF THE BUFALINO FAMILY

Russell Bufalino's agonizing efforts to avoid deportation and the struggle for power in the Teamsters union. Frank Fitzsimmons replaced imprisoned Jimmy Hoffa as leader of the Union, and he collaborated in a very profitable way with organized crime, being at the same time close to President Nixon. Thanks to the Union's pension funds, the Mafia had the opportunity to get credit flows and invest massively in the entertainment industry, making Las Vegas the entertainment capital. However, Hoffa was released in 1971 and was determined to get the Teamsters' control back. Bufalino advised him to retire and tried to protect him, but he turned hostile to him after a Time article we'll see. Hoffa mysteriously disappeared in 1975.

The Struggle for the Teamsters' Control

Having arrived in his mid-sixties, by the late 1960s, Russell Bufalino was still fighting against the government, which, on its part, was fighting to kick him out of the United States. In 1967, his attorney, Jack Wasserman, claimed that Bufalino was the victim of illegal wiretapping from the FBI, so the whole process was illegitimate and should be stopped or dismissed. He had added that by deporting his client to Italy, they could send him to his death, as Bufalino's life would be in danger in his country of origin. The Board of Immigration Appeals rejected those claims on June 5, 1967, and denied Bufalino's request, insisting on the deportation decision. Wasserman reacted with another appeal.

This deportation saga was long and, even worse, expensive, as Bufalino had to pay an army of lawyers to face his tough legal wars. That was the case also because the deportation case was not the only one. In 1969, he was indicted and charged for plotting to transport tens of television sets to Pittston from Buffalo. The televisions were color sets and cost $35,000; the problem was that they were stolen. Two more persons were accused with him, members of Stefano Magaddino's crime family. Bufalino had to deal with other charges, too, but he always got clean without severe consequences.

In the same years, Bufalino continued to be very present in criminal and legitimate businesses alike. Apart from his essential Mafia operations like extortion, gambling, prostitution, and loan-sharking, he earned a tribute of 10% from every aspiring entrepreneur in "his" area. And he owned legitimate car junkyards, hotels, and, of course, his dress shops and garment factories. Also, he facilitated many hotel owners in the Pocono Mountains to get loans, which is not clear if it was entirely legal.

But. Perhaps the main sector of the Bufalino crime family's business operations was, by this time, labor racketeering. Bufalino earned money off the loans that were made from the Teamsters Union pensions fund. That was serious business, so Bufalino and the family had to be very careful with Jimmy Hoffa and keep an eye on him.

Jimmy Hoffa had been convicted in 1964 and was finally brought to prison in 1967 at Lewisburg, Pennsylvania. So, in charge of the Teamsters union was now Frank Fitzsimmons, who was previously the chief lieutenant of Hoffa. Fitzsimmons had a different approach from Hoffa in managing the Union, as he was a conciliator and tried to find common grounds satisfying all parties and not confrontational like Hoffa. That means he was also more political and grasped that the Union had to be decentralized as an organization if it wanted to remain influential. Hoffa had maintained a kind of dictatorship in his way of making decisions. Fitzsimmons changed that, giving much more autonomy to local directors of the Union, the regional leaders.

That also brought changes in the way the Union contacted and collaborated with the mob. With Hoffa in charge, the rest of the Union's directors had a secondary role, to say the least. Hoffa himself was in direct contact with Mafia bosses and members and did everything by himself. On the contrary, Fitzsimmons's new decentralized structure collaborated with organized crime at the local levels. He determined that when a Mafia boss wanted a favor or money, he should just talk to the regional representative of the Teamsters union in his area; there was no need to contact the Teamster's national leadership.

Hoffa did not like these new arrangements made by Fitzsimmons. Actually, he was like really mad. However, Fitzsimmons got it right with the ones that mattered the most: the mob bosses. Organized crime leaders, in fact, liked the new direction given by Fitzsimmons, as access to funds would be easier and more direct. Bufalino was one of them. Indeed, thanks to Fitzsimmons's decentralizing reforms, the Teamsters Union began lending money to an unparalleled extent.

A lot of that money went to Las Vegas casinos owned and controlled by the mob, which, after the fall of Cuba to the Communists, concentrated the whole of entertainment investment to Las Vegas—strange twists of history. Without Fidel Castro's Communist revolution and then dictatorship, Havana would have become arguably more Las Vegas than Las Vegas, as it also had the beach. Castro's rise to power and the end of Mafia investment in Cuba brought all that money and investment in the casino industry exclusively toward Las Vegas, creating the entertainment capital of the United States and the world there.

There was one more reason for the Mafia's favor toward Fitzsimmons. That was the fact that he was working on creating links with President Richard Nixon, even though in 1968, the Teamsters Union had officially endorsed Hubert Humphrey, the candidate of the Democratic Party. President Nixon was a pragmatic and realist politician, so he understood that the Teamsters' support would be useful to him. He was open to forgetting their previous political preference and even, most importantly, giving Hoffa a pardon if they backed him up and came to his camp.

Fitzsimmons did not drop the opportunity and fueled Nixon and the attorney general, John Mitchell, with money flows. Under Nixon, Mitchell and the Justice Department focused on other issues. The Mafia investigations and prosecutions faded, and the mob had the chance to grow again fast, without big obstacles.

Nevertheless, on October 7, 1971, after years of appeals and a tactic of delaying deportation, the U.S. Court of Appeals rejected another Bufalino's appeal against his deportation and ordered him to leave the United States and go to Italy immediately. Yet, there was always another appeal in the law world, and Bufalino would, of course, use it together with every other possible option. He was definitely not going to give up.

Two and a half months later, as the 1971 Christmas was coming, and the cities' streets were full of decorations, Santa Clauses, and happy children, Hoffa was released from the Lewisburg jail after almost five years on December 23. President Nixon had reduced his initial sentence, which was thirteen years in prison, because Hoffa had been a model prisoner, and he needed to assist his wife, who meanwhile suffered a heart attack.

Of course, everything couldn't be so idyllic and magical for Hoffa. In order to set up a morally and legally supportable release, the government forbade Hoffa to engage in any kind of labor organization management, direct or indirect, until March 1980. That was more than eight years in the future, and Hoffa, by the end of 1971, was nearly 59 years old. So, the release was almost also a forced retirement. That should be good news to Hoffa, as he had told the parole board that if released, he would spend the rest of his days teaching and playing with his grandchildren. Naturally, that was a lie. Hoffa became furious with Fitzsimmons, as he learned about the forbidden clause of the deal only after he was released.

Hoffa thought that Fitzsimmons and the Teamsters leaders had betrayed him as rats that were devouring that which he himself had created. He was the one that made the Teamsters a national big deal, and now he was cut off in order for Fitzsimmons, the chief rodent, to take charge of the Union. Hoffa thought he was the owner of the Teamsters, the king, and that he had to be its leader for all his life. Also, he thought that without that deal, he would have been released by 1974 for good behavior anyway, and in that case, he could return to office as President of the Union in 1976. It was clear to him that Fitzsimmons made that deal only to neutralize him and grab the

Teamsters' presidency. The fact that they kept the forbidding clause secret from him until he was released perhaps proves that his accusations toward Fitzsimmons weren't wrong or entirely wrong.

Fitzsimmons had grown strong on his own during the years Hoffa was imprisoned. He had also established a really close relationship with President Nixon, and that gave him all the momentum and power he could wish for. He did not want to be seen as the temporary replacement of Hoffa anymore, but become the official President of the Teamsters Union. Indeed, supported by the President, who even surprisingly visited the Teamsters 1971 convention in Fitzsimmons's support, Fitzsimmons won the Union's election. Then, in 1972, he repaid the favor by supporting Nixon's reelection with all the might the Teamsters could have. The partnership between the President and the labor union became even stronger, and Fitzsimmons's post and leadership were secure and consolidated even more.

Yet, Hoffa would not bow down so easily. He contacted Bufalino and told him that he had the intention to hit back at Fitzsimmons and get revenge for what he felt was his overthrowing from the leadership of the Teamsters. He was determined to get the Union back and become its President once more. But Hoffa's time has passed. Nobody needed him anymore, as Fitzsimmons, with his reforms and his friendship with the President of the United States, was a hell of a better option for being the leader of the big labor union instead of the ex-convict Hoffa, who was much tighter in the management of the Union's finances, and at this point couldn't even dream of being a close friend to the U.S. President either.

Bufalino was so happy to suck off the pension funds thanks to Fitzsimmons policies, so he responded to Hoffa that instead of planning his revenge and return to power, he should better take the

$1.7 million of his Teamster pension and truly do what he had said to the judges that he was going to do if released by prison: play with his grandchildren and teach them for the rest of his life. It was a closed case. Bufalino had already years ago taken his cousin William away from Hoffa, as there was no business future there. He understood Hoffa's anger, but things were as they were, and everybody was winning with the new situation. Hoffa was not in a bad position, frankly. He could just take the money and have fun, free, away from stressful situations.

The problem for Russell Bufalino was definitely something entirely different: his deportation proceedings. His group of lawyers, guided by Wasseman, argued the last appeal Bufalino had the right to do on November 27, 1972. The decision of the Board of Immigration Appeals was again the same as on January 30, 1973, when it ordered him definitively to leave the United States. The judges added that his attorney had been in charge of the techniques that had kept the petitioner in the United States, although he purposefully and fraudulently claimed U.S. citizenship.

Yet, team Bufalino had another secret weapon. A suitcase containing one million dollars was sent to Italy, and perhaps it helped the Italian authorities to determine that Russell Bufalino had such a bad character that Italy couldn't accept him in the country. That decision made the U.S. court decision inapplicable, and Bufalino stayed in the United States.

Meanwhile, on July 16, 1972, Tommy Eboli, the boss of the Genovese family after Vito Genovese's death three years before, was shot to death while walking to get into his car on a street in Brooklyn. The Eboli assassination left the leadership of the Genovese family vacant, and Bufalino took control of this crime family, at least until the Commission came up with an official successor.

By the mid-1970s, Bufalino was more powerful than ever. In his 70s but still perfectly active, he had more power than even the FBI could imagine for a gangster who lived in the Scranton suburbs and wasn't a member of the Commission. The Bufalino crime family in Northeastern Pennsylvania had, by that time, more than fifty members and was ever-growing. But there was much more for him.

First, he had control of the Genovese family, and through this, he was in constant contact with the other four Mafia New York families. Then, in July 1974, Stefano Magaddino died at age eighty-two after a heart attack. With his mentor gone, who was also a member of the Commission and boss of his crime family in upstate New York for more than half a century, only Bufalino himself could maintain the Magaddino family united and secure their interests in Buffalo and in other regions.

In this way, Bufalino was essentially the boss of three Mafia families. His own in Pennsylvania, the Magaddino family in Buffalo, and the Genovese family in New York. A real crime empire that made him even stronger and bigger than other bosses and law enforcement agents could think. Bufalino liked that. He had no interest in becoming a bombastic capo, a leading member of the Commission. He preferred the role of the powerful man behind the scenes.

However, if someone thought that Bufalino's problems were over and he could finally enjoy his wealth and power, they would be completely wrong.

Hoffa Goes Out of Control

In April 1973, Jimmy Hoffa went public about his intention to get control of the Teamsters union back while he was at a banquet in Washington, D.C. He had already talked about that on other occasions in closed circles of supporters, like during the dinner for his 60th birthday in New Jersey at the Latin Casino in Cherry Hill. Old buddy Russell Bufalino was there, but Fitzsimmons was not, saying he already had another commitment.

By the spring of 1973, it was more than a year after Hoffa's release, and he had done everything he could to convince others about his social goodwill. Also, he vigorously supported Richard Nixon for the presidency, aligned with the position of the Teamsters. With all that, Hoffa hoped that he could challenge and remove the ban that forbade him to run for the Union's presidency or any other office. He claimed that the secret clause in the deal for the President's pardon and his release was unconstitutional; the President didn't have the authority to put such clauses in order to give his pardon. Also, Hoffa suggested that the clause could have violated his right to freedom of speech, protected by the First Amendment, and he argued that it wasn't included in the sentence that had condemned him to prison in the first place.

In the same period, Hoffa played a strong card in obtaining an affidavit from John Mitchell, the attorney general and now director of the Committee to Reelect the President. A suitcase with around $300,000 delivered to Mitchell by Frank Sheeran obviously helped in that. After the delivery, Mitchell stated that Nixon had nothing to do with the clause that included the aforementioned restrictions for Hoffa and that no one in the Justice Department had initiated or suggested them as a term for the President's pardon of Hoffa.

A few months later, in February 1974, Hoffa began an all-out attack. Feeling again in shape and confident that he would have the permission to run for the Teamsters presidency, he said openly that Fitzsimmons was not the right leader for the Union. In March, he prepared his lawsuit arguing that since President Nixon and Attorney General Mitchell hadn't imposed the restrictions, as the affidavit stated, they were invalid because nobody else except for the two had the authority to impose them. Hoffa also declared that the restrictions clause had been kept secret by him and that if he had known, he would have disagreed. Nevertheless, in July 1974, a Washington D.C. federal judge rejected Hoffa's lawsuit on the grounds that the President had signed the pardon with the restrictions clause, so the restrictions couldn't be invalid. Hoffa naturally made an appeal.

After Nixon's resignation, in the autumn of 1974, Hoffa made the statement that after he won the election for the Teamsters residence in 1976, he would call in pension loans given by Fitzsimmons. That would be his revenge against his former friend and associate.

Many Mafia bosses were concerned and nervous to hear the news, as those loans were used for the construction of casinos in Las Vegas, and members of several crime families had majority interests in those casino projects. One of the bosses who was concerned about Hoffa's intentions was Bufalino. So, he told Sheeran to arrange a meeting between himself and Hoffa at the bar restaurant Broadway Eddie's in Philadelphia. Apart from him, Angelo Bruno would be there.

During the dinner, Bufalino told Hoffa that it would be better if he abandoned his plans to run again for the presidency of the Teamsters Union. However, Hoffa responded that he was determined to be a candidate, as he strongly desired revenge against

Fitzsimmons, kicking him out of the Teamsters' leadership. We have seen earlier in the book that Bufalino used to make his point only once and then to hear the response from the other part, considering it final. In this particular case, he insisted, arguing for a second time that it would be better for everyone if Hoffa changed his decision and forgot about running for the Teamsters presidency. Hoffa did not accept Bufalino's suggestion.

In the following period, Bufalino, through Sheeran, tried his best to convince Hoffa to change his mind and then to protect him from the not-so-friendly intentions of many people in the mob, like Tony Provenzano, who hated Hoffa because of their previous beef. Bufalino had known Hoffa for thirty years and had collaborated profitably with him for a long time, and he believed that he was honest. He rejected the notions about Hoffa cooperating with law enforcement that some people, even during the Teamsters convention in April 1975, were spreading. Bufalino stood against these kinds of rumors and accusations. Nevertheless, Hoffa's position became always more precarious and dangerous, as gradually more mobsters considered him a pain in the ass, to say the least, or an all-out enemy to be eliminated without any more time wasting.

Time Magazine Convinces Bufalino He Has Had Enough

Bufalino changed his mind about Hoffa after, on June 9, 1975, Time magazine published an article in which Bufalino, along with James Plumeri and Salvatore Granello, were mentioned as cooperating with the CIA in 1961 as spies in Cuba, in preparation for the Bay of Pigs failed operation.

Bufalino and the others were mentioned literally as "Mafiosi," and Bufalino was pointed out as the mob boss in Scranton, while Plumeri and Granello as lesser fry. The article wrote that the three mobsters had left Cuba $450,000 and that they wanted Castro to be overthrown in order to get the money back and also return to profit from their Havana businesses that's why they had cooperated with the CIA to no avail.

That was too much for Bufalino, who had always been very careful in remaining away from the public eyes and was committed to playing behind the scenes. It was obvious to him that the source of the information given to the Time was Hoffa.

On the evening of July 30, Jimmy Hoffa went missing. Two hundred FBI agents would participate in the investigations of his disappearance. That afternoon, he was supposed to have a meeting with Tony Provenzano and another known mobster, Tony Giacalone, from Detroit. They were supposed to eat together near Bloomfield Township at the Machus Red Fox Restaurant. The 1974 Pontiac Grand DeVille of Hoffa, color green, was indeed there. But nobody knew anything about its owner. Provenzano and Giacalone denied that they had an appointment with Hoffa, claiming alibis.

The FBI formed a list in which Provenzano, Sheeran, and Bufalino were the most important suspects. Other names involved in the investigations were Charles O'Brien, who used to call himself Hoffa's foster son, and Salvatore "Sally Bugs" Briguglio, who was a business agent of the Teamsters in Detroit. And more. The FBI agents were certain that around 2:30 p.m. on July 30, Hoffa had entered a car with O'Brien, Briguglio, and others at that precise location. What happened next remained a mystery, and it would be so for almost 30 years, as we shall see in the next chapter.

Back in 1975, the authorities continued to press hard against Bufalino, trying to find evidence of his involvement in Hoffa's disappearance and, as the FBI agents believed, murder. Bufalino was called to testify in front of a grand jury in December of that year, just like the other names mentioned above and more. William Bufalino, their lawyer, told them to take the Fifth Amendment, that is, the right not to respond because they could say something that would incriminate them. So, nobody answered anything.

But the pressure continued, and in June 1976, New York law enforcement investigators called him to the Consulate Hotel in New York and interviewed him on his shops and plants in the garment industry, which were much less than in the past. Bufalino now was owner or co-owner in only six of them, instead of the tens he once had. The investigators had found a not-so-clear connection of Bufalino to Fair Frox Inc., which was on Fifth Avenue in New York. He responded that from 1972 onward, he was employed at Fair Frox and got a regular paycheck. In fact, there wasn't much to tell about Bufalino's garment business, and it was obvious to him that the whole investigation and interview were part of a plan orchestrated by the FBI to put more psychological pressure on him and break him in order to make him talk about the Hoffa case. Similar tactics were probably followed with other suspects as well.

CHAPTER 7

THE BUFALINO FAMILY IN INTRIGUING AND MYSTERY STORIES OF NATIONAL INTEREST (AND BEYOND)

We delve into the fascinating making of "The Godfather" and the real Mafia's role in this, especially how Russell Bufalino stopped the initial protests and supported the production, actively helping Marlon Brando interpret his classic family boss role under Francis Ford Coppola's direction. Second, we discuss the mystery of Jimmy Hoffa's disappearance, which was solved almost thirty years later. Last but not least, a brief look at the ultimate Mafia conspiracy theory: Frank Sheeran's notion that Bufalino was involved in the assassination of John F. Kennedy.

Russell Bufalino and *The Godfather*

While Russell Bufalino was locked in his battle with the government concerning his deportation from the United States, in 1969, Mario Puzo's "The Godfather" was published and had enormous success. The novel, which talked about a fictional Italian-American crime boss from Sicily named Vito Corleone, became a New York Times bestseller and stayed on the book list for sixty-seven straight weeks. Right away, Paramount Pictures started working to make a movie based on the novel with Francis Ford Coppola as director and Marlon Brando in the first role as Vito Corleone.

Of course, we all know this is a classic film, as well as its two sequels. And we can't even imagine the Mafia and that historical era of organized crime in the United States without bringing into mind the magical touch of Coppolla, Marlon Brando's (and Al Pacino's, and Robert De Niro's) brilliant performance, and Nino Rota's evocative music. But the first reaction of the Italian-American community and of the real Mafia toward Puzo's novel and the possibility of a movie based on it entering the 1970s was not so positive.

On the contrary, it was quickly formed the Italian-American Civil Rights League which accused the FBI of being discriminatory against Italian Americans. In June 1970, it rallied more than 100,000 people to protest in New York. Feeling that the film would be yet another chapter in the literature's and cinema's tendency to present the Italians in a negative and repulsive way, many Italian-Americans joined the league, which soon came to have branches in several cities. The founder and leader of the league was Joe Colombo, the boss of the New York Colombo crime family.

Soon, another rally was organized in New York at the Madison Square Garden, and Colombo claimed that the league would use the link with the Teamsters union to cancel the production of the film.

Also, Frank Sinatra was not happy with the novel and the movie's production. Probably, you'll remember the Johnny Fontaine character in "The Godfather," the famous singer loved by many girls, who was connected with the Corleone crime family and gained fame and wealth thanks to the family's promotion and support. Well, that character was inspired by Sinatra and his close relationship with Sam Giancana, the crime boss of Chicago. The famous singer did not like the prospect of a film and tried to cancel the production any way he could.

Colombo got something to go. The word "Mafia" was removed after he requested so, and then after he reviewed the script, he changed his mind and position toward the movie. The protests faded away. Russell Bufalino had very much something to do with it, as together with other Mafia bosses, they ordered the turmoil to stop and Colombo to make peace with the producers.

The bosses and, most of all, Bufalino saw that, in fact, the movie was not that defamatory for the Italians, but it could be seen as an immigrant Italian success story in the United States. The violent and gangster-like elements were secondary; the primary effect of the film would be the presentation of a family with humble immigrant origins that managed to become wealthy and powerful in America.

Coppola's version of "The Godfather" was not a vulgar film about the blind and brutal violence of ugly Italians who terrorized society and oppressed their families but a high-quality drama to be put among the great tragedies of theatrical and cinematographic history. Also, the Corleone family was not a gang of thieves and murderers but more of a corporation that sold entertainment, corrupting politicians and law enforcement agents just as part of the business. When Bufalino was informed about what that young director from Detroit named Coppola was working on, he was excited. He assumed an extremely positive attitude toward the production of the film.

The film gave for the first time a deeper view of what the Italian Mafia was, pointing out that that kind of organized crime corresponded with a form of social organization and rules. Of course, it was a primitive and underdeveloped social form with a lot of violence, something like a relic of past centuries that somehow had survived in the modern extended societies organized on the rule of law and not the rule of family blood and paternal hierarchy. Yet, that view gave back to the Mafiosi their humanity, and intelligent mob bosses like Bufalino understood that.

Bufalino's interest and support made him a factor in the production itself and, precisely, the casting. He was the one who promoted Al Lattieri for the role of Virgil "the Turk" Sollozzo, the crime boss who tries to have Vito Corleone assassinated in the film. Lettieri was a real gangster. He was associated with Tommy and Patsy Eboli, the two acting leaders of the Genovese crime family during the 1960s when Vito Genovese was in jail after the Apalachin fiasco; they became official bosses after Genovese died in 1969. Lettieri worked for his Eboli "uncles," and he also became an actor, playing in a television movie in 1964. Bufalino promoted him to a role in The Godfather, and Lettieri invited and hosted Marlon Brando, Al Pacino, and James Caan to the house of Patsy Eboli in Fort Lee, New Jersey. Later, Patsy Eboli himself helped the production as an advisor on the set near Coppola.

Lattieri, Eboli, and Bufalino were not the only real gangsters who were involved in the making of The Godfather. One of them, Lenny Montana, is Luca Brasi in the movie, a very brief but emblematic role.

Russell Bufalino visited the set several times, and he hung out particularly with Marlon Brando, also in his trailer in Little Italy in Manhattan. It was a rough time for him, as he was battling against his deportation, and we can imagine that The Godfather was a comfort for him. On the other hand, Marlon Brando had the chance to get many takeaways from a Mafia boss's thinking and acting, which helped him pull away his iconic performance, which gave him the Oscar for Best Actor, while the film won the Best Picture award. Marlon Brando's performance was inspired by Russell Bufalino's style, at least to a certain extent, a charismatic imitation of him. So, if someone wants to see Russell Bufalino in action, they can watch The Godfather again—just keep in mind that Marlon Brando was way more handsome.

There is another Bufalino-related story in the making of The Godfather. Coppola had chosen the singer Vic Damone for the role of Johnny Fontaine, but the singer Al Martino really wanted it. He tried so hard to get it that he organized a big party with showgirls and booze in Las Vegas, on which he spent approximately $25,000, where he invited Coppola and his collaborators in the production. Martino's partying attempt to get his hands on the role failed miserably, but he had another card in his pocket. He was connected to the real Mafia, and Bufalino was his godfather. Martino begged Bufalino to help him, and a few days later, Damone coincidentally quit the role, and Martino finally got it.

This story is ironic as Johnny Fountaine does exactly the same thing in the movie, asking his godfather, Vito Corleone, to convince a film producer to pick him for a movie. Fortunately, in the real story, the director was left out of that, and there was no cut horse head, at least as far as we know.

The Truth About Jimmy Hoffa's Disappearance

Jimmy Hoffa's disappearance and presumed death in 1975 were destined to be clarified only nearly thirty years later when, before dying, Frank Sheeran finally confessed that he had indeed killed Hoffa so many years before, as the FBI had always suspected. Sheeran made the confession when he was 83 years old to the author

Charles Brandt, who wrote his biography titled "I Heard You Paint Houses," published in 2004, the year after Sheeran's death. The other suspects, who were thought to have collaborated with the murder, were Russell Bufalino, Tony Provenzano, Sally Briguglio, Anthony Giancala, and Steve and Tom Andretta. Law enforcement was right but always lacked evidence.

According to Sheeran's story, after Bufalino decided that Hoffa had to die joining his fellow gangsters on this matter, withdrawing his support for Hoffa because of the Time article we talked about, he put up a plan. On August 1, 1975, while Russell Bufalino and Frank Sheeran were in the latter's black Lincoln driving to Detroit for the wedding of Bill Bufalino's daughter, they stopped near Lake Erie in Port Clinton, Ohio, around a hundred miles from the city. They left their wives there at a diner for a break, saying that they had a job to take care of and they would return later to continue the trip. That didn't feel strange because Bufalino used to make similar stops and jump to quick works.

Then Bufalino and Sheeran drove to a small airport that had an airstrip with grass. Sheeran took a single-engine airplane that awaited him and flew to Detroit. Sheeran arrived at an airfield north of Detroit named Pontiac, and there he took a car that was left there for him with the keys under the mat, a gray Ford, and he went to a house in the city. There, he met Sally Briguglio and the two Andretta brothers, and Chuckie O'Brien was on his way to get there, too. Jimmy Hoffa raised the latter, and that would be his only role in the plan, making Hoffa feel comfortable and safe. O'Brien didn't know that the meeting with Hoffa would end with the death of him. Also, Sheeran would make Hoffa feel comfortable and safe.

After O'Brien arrived, he, Sheeran, and Briguglio left with a maroon Mercury car, and they went to meet Hoffa at a restaurant, where he reacted with anger as he waited for Provenzano and Giacalone for hours. O'Brien introduced him to Briguglio, and Briguglio told him that he was there with Provenzano. Then, Hoffa saw that Sheeran was also there, still inside the car. Sheeran told him he was with his "friend," meaning Bufalino, and explained that they were late because of some delays.

Hoffa indeed felt calmer because of O'Brien and Sheeran's presence, and he agreed to get into the car, dropping his guard. Soon, they were back at the brick house. O'Brien and Briguglio remained in the car and drove away. Sheeran was the only one who accompanied Hoffa to the house, where Hoffa expected to see Provenzano, Giacalone, and Bufalino. But there was neither of them. After they walked up the stairs and entered the house, Hoffa realized that the house was totally empty. Knowing what that meant, he tried to get out the fastest he could. But Sheeran was well prepared for the moment and an expert in those kinds of situations. His gun was already loaded, and he shot Hoffa in the back of the head two times before he could reach the door and get out.

Sheeran left with the gray Ford and returned directly to the Pontiac airstrip, where the pilot was waiting for him, and he boarded the same single-engine aircraft. After an hour, he was back to the airport of Port Clinton. He caught up with Bufalino, who was waiting for him in the car, and they returned to the diner to pick up their wives. Then, they finally drove to Detroit and went to Bill Bufalino's daughter's wedding.

Bufalino later said to Sheeran that the Andretta brothers had cleaned the house of Hoffa's body and blood and took his body to an incinerator. Hoffa's body was never found for the simple reason that it didn't exist, as it was cremated that same day.

Hoffa's murder is a cruel and raw example of the coldness and precision those gangsters used to act, capable of organizing a similar sequence of actions in the middle of a happy road trip to a wedding without anyone noticing anything strange.

Related to JFK's Assassination?

Closing this chapter with the most intriguing and mysterious stories of the Bufalino crime family on a national level and beyond, it's time to reveal that the most shocking information by the time the FBI was investigating Bufalino was not included in Chapter 5, where we saw in detail the battle between law enforcement and the Bufalino crime family during the 1960s. Instead, it is definitely one that relates to JFK's assassination.

The FBI came to know in September 1963, around two months before the shooting in Dallas that shocked the world, that Bufalino had some contacts with a person who was in Mexico, initially in Guadalajara. Later, in November 1963, he received many phone calls from Mexico City. The FBI didn't know, though, that in parallel, Jimmy Hoffa called Frank Sheeran, telling him to visit Bufalino at his house in Kingston, Pennsylvania.

Bufalino guided him to visit their Brooklyn pals, pick up a box there, and transport personally with his car to Baltimore. The Brooklyn pals were Genovese Mafia family members. Among them was Tony Provenzano, a captain of the family, who was also a Hoffa's colleague, as he managed a Teamster local in New Jersey.

When Sheeran got to Brooklyn and met him, Provenzano gave him a bag and told him to go to Baltimore and meet a pilot there. Sheeran never checked what the bag had inside, but he knew how guns in a bag felt, as he had earlier transported guns on other occasions. He was sure that inside the bag were three rifles.

Sheeran went to Baltimore, gave the package, and immediately returned to Pennsylvania. President John F. Kennedy was killed only a few days after that. Yes, Sheeran believed that the guns he carried in Baltimore were, for sure, used to shoot the president.

Sheeran added that a week after the president was killed, he visited Bufalino at the Vesuvio restaurant, and the Mafia boss was delighted.

CHAPTER 8

THE DISINTEGRATION

In the book's closing chapter, we'll see how, in the late 1970s, law enforcement found a way to successfully bring Mafia bosses like Tony Provenzano and Russell Bufalino to the court of law and in prison. Many members of the Bufalino crime family were imprisoned or died in the following years. In 1989, Bufalino suffered a stroke. Control of the Bufalino family passed to Billy D'Elia, who tried to expand its activities and territorial presence. We'll follow D'Elia's attempts after Bufalino's death and the final disintegration of the Bufalino crime family.

The Strange End of an Era

When, in August 1976, Johnny Roselli was found dead with evident signs of torture in a drum in a Miami bay, it was clear that the Church Committee could not complete its report on the relationship between organized crime and the CIA. It was the third murder of a person who testified to the committee after those of Giancana and—according to the committee—Hoffa. The committee delivered its report as it was by then.

In parallel, the investigations into Hoffa's disappearance could not bear fruit. The evidence was not enough to bring someone to the court of law, and as we saw, it would take nearly thirty years before the truth came out after the confession of near-death Frank Sheeran. There is always another solution, though, as we know since the famous Al Capone case. If the government can't catch the outlaws for their major criminal activities, the government can always hope to find a weak point in other criminal activities it chases them for.

In the case of Tony Provenzano, the boss of the Genovese family and a Teamsters union leader for years, that weak point the law enforcement was able to find was the murder of an official of the Teamsters back in 1961. So, Provenzano went to trial and was convicted in prison in 1978. Sheeran was first indicted in 1980 on two murders and a series of other cases, but he was found innocent, and he finally was convicted in 1981 in thirty-two years in prison for labor racketeering. On his part, Giacalone was found guilty of income tax fraud and convicted to ten years in prison. In the case of Briguglio, in the end, the authorities did not have to prove their suspicions that he was involved in the 1961 murder that condemned Provenzano, as someone shot him to death in March 1978 in New York.

Russell Bufalino Finally in Jail

For Russell Bufalino, the case the law enforcement managed to use to finally lock him in jail was the strangest of all. It all began when Jack Napoli, a bartender from Brooklyn, used Bufalino's name to come in contact with a jewelry dealer who had some stolen diamonds. Then Napoli paid $25,000 to buy the diamonds but with a bounced check. When Bufalino came to know that a bartender had used his name to buy stolen diamonds he didn't even have the money for, Bufalino went mad.

Napoli understood that he was in trouble with what he had done, and he immediately went to the FBI, asking for protection. The FBI agents did not lose the opportunity and told him he could help them a lot if he accepted to be wiretapped during his meeting with Bufalino, that they knew it was about to come. Indeed, the old don was furious and called Napoli to his Vesuvio restaurant to explain himself and order him to give back the diamonds, or else he was going to kill him with his own hands. Bufalino told Napoli: "I'm going to kill you, cocksucker, and I'm going to do it myself, and I'm going to jail just for you."

Bufalino was famous for his cool temper, never losing control and talking too much, and that was a factor in his success as a Mafia boss. But at that time, he was extremely angry with Napoli for using his name in that way, and he was for once caught off guard by law enforcement, as they had everything on tape.

In this way, on October 27, 1976, FBI agents arrested Bufalino at his home in Kingston and took him to a preliminary hearing in Wilkes-Barre. He was released after he paid a $50,000 bond, and that was just the beginning. The only solution for Bufalino was for Napoli to be killed and, thus, not to testify.

In September 1976, Bufalino was at the Rainbow Room in Manhattan just after he had attended Frank Sinatra's sold-out concert at the Westchester Premier Theater, the second after the one in April. The Westchester Premier Theater was a successful hall that earned hundreds of thousands of dollars for its owners. Still, it was under federal investigation, as it was owned by two New York gangsters, Gregory DePalma and Richard Fusco, and a securities salesman named Eliot Weisman. It was opened a year earlier with a concert by Diana Ross. Also, Carlo Gambino, boss of one of the New York Mafia families, had offered financial help for this luxury facility to open, with a 10% interest rate. Not surprisingly, mobsters from all over the United States were there for the Sinatra concert that night. One of them was Jimmy "the Weasel" Frattiano, who at the time was acting boss of the Los Angeles mob.

Frattiano had participated in ten murders in his criminal career, and in 1977, he would be charged with the murder of a union official named Danny Green. Green was killed in Cleveland with a bomb under his car, and Frattiano was the one who had introduced to the Cleveland mob the hitman that killed Green. Frattiano agreed to enter the Witness Protection Program and cooperate with the police as an informant under the term that he would serve no more than five years in prison; in fact, he would serve just twenty-one months. As a protected witness, Frattiano mentioned to the agents that Russell Bufalino planned to kill Jack Napoli.

After the Sinatra concert, Frattiano met Bufalino at the Rainbow Room in Manhattan, and Bufalino spoke to him in confidence about the grand jury that was investigating him. Bufalino told Frattiano that he needed to take out someone, i.e., Napoli, who was about to testify against him. The reason why Bufalino chose Frattiano to talk for the job is impressive. Thanks to the amazing connections he had in the government, Bufalino knew that Napoli was under FBI protection as the owner of a pork store in Walnut Creek, California. Walnut Creek was near the home of Frattiano in San Francisco. Frattiano was the best person to help with that problem.

Bufalino and Frattiano talked for around twenty minutes at the Rainbow Room, and they gave an appointment for two days later at the Vesuvio restaurant. There was also Mike Rizzitello, another prominent member of the Los Angeles crime family. Frattiano agreed to do the job for Bufalino, and after he returned to San

Francisco, he began looking for Napoli at Walnut Creek. But Napoli was nowhere to be found.

In May 1977, Frattiano went again to New York for a Frank Sinatra concert at the Westchester Premier Theater. After the concert, he went again to the Vesuvio restaurant in Manhattan with Rizzitello to see Bufalino. Frattiano told Bufalino that he couldn't find Napoli, and the latter responded that, obviously, Napoli had left town, so he had to find another way to get to him and take him out. In fact, nobody knew where Napoli was at the time since he had fled from Walnut Creek owing $3,000 to Wells Fargo Bank.

Later that year, Frattiano was arrested on the murder of Danny Green and many other charges, as already mentioned, and he agreed to cooperate with the FBI to reduce his sentence. Frattiano testified that Bufalino had asked him to kill Napoli, and on October 21, 1977, Bufalino was convicted to four years in jail. Ironically, it was his attempt to prevent Napoli from testifying that provoked the testimony that incriminated him through Frattiano.

Bufalino appealed, but the appeal was rejected. He stayed for six weeks at the Metropolitan Correctional Center in New York in August and September 1978, and the federal judge Morris Lasker gave him permission to celebrate the anniversary of his wedding, which was the 50th, in Pennsylvania. When he returned to New York after this furlough, initially, they sent him to the federal prison in Springfield, Missouri. Then, Bufalino was finally transferred to the Federal Institution at Danbury, Connecticut.

In that medium-security prison, Bufalino had a quite calm permanence, and he liked to play cards, to be more specific, pinochle. At the same time, he continued to supervise his crime family and his businesses. Everything had been discussed at the party for his wedding anniversary at his hotel at Howard Johnson. There were mobsters from Northeastern Pennsylvania, New York, Philadelphia, Buffalo, and other places, and apart from drinking and having fun, they talked about business, and it was determined that Bufalino would continue to be the head of his family even from inside prison, with Edward Sciandra, James Osticco, and Billy D'Elia acting like underbosses following his orders.

Bufalino was released on May 8, 1981, but not for long. Soon, he was put again on trial, where he was convicted to fifteen more years in prison, as the prosecutor Nathanial Akerman received from the judge permission to play the wiretap with Bufalino's death threat to Jack Napoli, and before the trial, the Pennsylvania Crime Commission published its report titled "A Decade of Organized Crime." During the previous years, Bufalino had also tried to get one of the other prisoners, Steven Fox, to find and kill Napoli after he was released from jail with parole. The evidence against Bufalino was now too much. Bufalino was out of the game and inside prison for good.

The Bufalino crime family members didn't know that in those years, the FBI had opened a special investigation named "Full-Time Surveillance of Members of the Russell A. Bufalino Family," commonly called RABFAM. Osticco was soon to be imprisoned as well, as he was sentenced to eight years in jail for fixing the trial of Louis DeNaples back in 1977. In July 1983, he was also charged, together with Casper Giumento, for having supplied dynamite to Frank Sheeran. Osticco would die in 1990 after he was released because of bad health two years earlier. On his part, consigliere Edward Sciandra was sentenced to two eighteen months in prison for not reporting income tax.

So, as the FBI noted during the 1980s, D'Elia became the undisputed leader of the Bufalino crime family, the one Russell Bufalino used to send his orders more often. In 1989, his close collaborator during those years, capo Anthony Guarnieri, was also sentenced for labor racketeering and many other charges to thirty years in jail. Frank Sheeran had been sentenced, too, after charges against him in 1980 of mail fraud, taking bribes, and, naturally, labor racketeering. His sentence was eighteen years in prison.

At the same time, all the older prominent members of the family were dead or imprisoned. Jack Parisi and Philip Medico died in December 1982 and February 1983, respectively. Soon after, the patriarch of the family, Steven LaTorre, who was one of the "Men of Montedoro" in the early 1900s, died in July 1984 at the age of 98. Casper "Cappy" Giumento would follow in March 1987. All of them died from natural causes, a sign that the time had passed for the crime family even though Russell Bufalino continued to be perfectly active even behind bars, now in his 80s.

That didn't mean that the Bufalino family faded away so easily. On the contrary, under D'Elia's leadership, the crime family collaborated closer with the Lucchese family in New York, established operations in Miami and Baltimore, and took control of the Edgewater Hotel and Casino in Laughlin, widening its reach in Nevada, as well. That move came after an agreement with Tony Spilotro, a violent gangster from Chicago who was portrayed in another famous gangster film, Martin Scorsese's "Casino" of 1995.

However, in December 1983, the FBI concluded the RABFAM investigation, considering that the Bufalino crime family had been essentially decimated, stating that at the time, its most important members had been convicted or in ongoing judicial proceedings.

In 1989, Russell Bufalino had a stroke and was transferred to the federal hospital in Springfield, Missouri. There, in a wheelchair, he finally retired, passing the next years doing lighter and calmer things, like playing bocce and attending mass regularly—that one had always been a central part of his life, not a retirement hobby. In Springfield, he also had the chance to reunite with Sheeran. He, too, transferred there because he suffered severely from arthritis.

Bufalino was released from prison in 1991, and they moved him to a nursing home in the Scranton area, where he lived his last years until his death of natural causes on February 25, 1994, at the age of 90. In those last years, he received many visitors who came to pay their respects to the great Mafia boss. There was also a ritual. Every visitor stopped and kissed the old gangster's feet after entering the room and approached the bed where he was lying.

The Bufalino Crime Family After Bufalino

As what went down as the "Bufalino crime family" had not started with Russell Bufalino, but even before he was born, it did not end with his death—not immediately. Indeed, what happened in 1994 was that Billy D'Elia, the acting boss for a while, became the actual boss of the family.

As mentioned earlier, D'Elia had made some pretty important moves under the supervision of Bufalino, expanding the family's reach and collaboration with other families of the country outside the previous geographical limits of action of the Bufalino family. After Bufalino's death, D'Elia tried to expand those limits and links even further. Under his leadership, the family worked with families in Philadelphia, southern Florida, New York, Pittsburgh, Los Angeles, Miami, Nevada, and even associates of Russian organized crime. In particular, D'Elia's collaboration with the Philadelfia

Mafia family was so close that when their boss, John Stanfa, was convicted and put in jail, he thought about appointing D'Elia as acting boss of the Philadelfia family.

At the same time, though, the Bufalino crime family, in fact, was shrinking. It was becoming weaker as its historical leaders and members were leaving the scene. D'Elia tried to give new impetus and vigor to the family, replacing members who left, were imprisoned, or died with new ones. However, his attempts did not have great success. The era of traditional organized crime and of the Bufalino family was in decline.

The family's activities during the D'Elia leadership included money laundering—a scheme in which many people were operating in the gambling and prostitution sectors, as well as corrupt politicians, of course, and the Russian "Mafia" participated.

So, on May 31, 2001, D'Elia, Jeanie Stanton, who was his mistress, and Thomas Joseph all had search warrants executed at their homes by the agents from the Criminal Investigation Division of the IRS, US Postal Inspectors, and the Pennsylvania State Police. The agents also searched the home of a certain Marranca, who was an informant working simultaneously for the FBI and the Pennsylvania State Police. Marranca would also testify to the Fourth Statewide Investigating Grand Jury against Louis DeNaples, focusing on DeNaples' connections to the Mafia as well as his control of the Mount Airy Casino.

After the warrants, on February 26, 2003, the New Jersey Division of Gaming Enforcement barred D'Elia from accessing the casinos in Atlantic City, New Jersey. This decision was made based on information that had been supplied by the Federal Bureau of Investigation and the Pennsylvania Crime Commission.

Exactly five years after the warrants of 2001, on May 31, 2006, D'Elia was charged on federal allegations of having laundered $600,000 in illicit narcotics revenues collected from a member of the Bufalino crime family who was based in Florida, as well as from other individuals. One of them was an associate of the Lucchese crime family whose name was Phillip "Fipper" Forgione. The charges were brought against D'Elia by the United States Department of Justice. During the time that D'Elia was out of jail on bond, he tried to convince an informant working for the United States Customs and Border Protection to kill a witness. As a result, he was detained in custody until he eventually pleaded guilty and was sentenced.

D'Elia entered a guilty plea to charges of witness tampering and money laundering in March of 2008. He was given a jail term of nine years for his crime. In the end, D'Elia's sentence was reduced because he became an informant and gave evidence against Louis DeNaples, the proprietor of the Mount Airy Casino Resort in the Pocono Mountains, cooperating with the government and testifying against him. As a reward for his assistance in the government investigation into DeNaples, D'Elia received a two-year reduction in the length of his sentence in the year 2010.

The Bufalino crime family has been considered extinct since around 2010, after its last boss, D'Elia, pleaded guilty and cooperated with law enforcement. In 2011, a former investigator of the Pennsylvania Crime Commission, named James Kanavy, said during an interview with the author Dave Janoski that there probably wasn't a crime family based in Northeastern Pennsylvania anymore. Any remnants of the Bufalino crime family at that point would be part of the remaining New York crime families.

CONCLUSION

There is no doubt that in the history of organized crime in the United States, the Bufalino crime family occupies a prominent position. For a long time, it operated in a secretive and enigmatic fashion, staying away from the main focus of law enforcement and maintaining a veil of silence, which many erroneously thought of as a weakness or lack of importance. The truth was that the Bufalino crime family had a long story going back to the beginning of the 20th century and became one of the most powerful families of organized crime during the years of Russell Bufalino's leadership.

Bufalino was so successful and reigned for so long among the leading figures of organized crime that his family is named after him, even though its origins go back to the very first years of the 1900s. However, thanks to Bufalino, the Northeastern Pennsylvania crime family expanded its influence beyond Pittston and Scranton, reaching a national broad level comparable to that of New York, Chicago, and Los Angeles crime families. Bufalino's businesses and investments would get Cuba, his influence and links to the most significant labor unions in the United States and the government, and his ability and financial power with the Italian authorities. The Bufalino crime family was involved in numerous criminal activities, such as loan-sharking, illegal gambling, extortion, prostitution, and labor racketeering.

On the other hand, the stronger it grew, the more the law enforcement took notice of the Bufalino family and intensified its attention to disintegrate it. In those years, law enforcement grew in power and capability much more than the crime families, thanks to the technological and tactical progress, which made surveillance and data collecting and analyzing much faster, more massive, and more efficient. Law enforcement agencies used wiretapping, task teams, informants, and intensive surveillance with many agents to deal with organized crime and bring its leaders and members to the court and behind the bars of prison.

Indeed, by the late 1970s and the 1980s, many leaders and associates of the Mafia paid for their criminal operations and actions. Organized crime, particularly in the Bufalino family, began to decline. Its fall would become evident and accelerated after Russell Bufalino died at 90 in 1994. After that date, the Bufalino crime family would never be the formidable criminal organization it once was, despite the efforts of its past leaders.

We could say, in conclusion, that the story of the Bufalino crime family represents an emblematic example of American organized crime's rise and fall, glory and demise. It shows how a quiet, calm, and friendly attitude can be deadly and efficient if accompanied by determination, cynicism, and precision. At the same time, on the other hand, it proves that not even the most effective, secretive, silent, and attentive criminal organizations can escape the clutches of law enforcement forever if it's determined, organized, well prepared, and uses the technological, psychological, and tactical scientific knowledge of our times.

From a point of view, it could be a raw and criminal implementation of the American dream. From another point of view, it could be the aspect of what didn't work well with the

American dream in the previous century, its bad version, a sickening way of pursuing the opportunity that America should represent. In any case, the history of the Bufalino crime family is part of an era and a society where success still used to pass often through violence and coercion, where organized crime was very present, even at the upper levels of society, business, and politics. An era we would prefer to have left behind, enjoying its fascinating aspects only through books, movies, and podcasts.

GLOSSARY

Aladena James Fratianno (1913-1993): Known as "Jimmy the Weasel," he was the acting boss of the Los Angeles crime family and spent over seven years in prison. He was accused of misrepresenting himself and conspiring towards Danny Greene's murder.

Angelo Bruno (1910-1980): He was a Sicilian-American mobster who was the boss of the Philadelphia crime family for two decades until his assassination in 1980. Born in Sicily, he immigrated to the U.S. and settled in South Philadelphia. Bruno was close to New York Gambino crime family boss Carlo Gambino and had a close relationship with mobster John Simone. He was married to Assunta "Sue" Maranca and owned various companies. Bruno's preference for conciliation over violence led to his assassination, sparking a mob war that claimed over 20 lives. His home was considered a historical landmark, but a committee ruled against it.

Anthony "Tony Jack" Joseph Giacalone (1919-2001): He was a Sicilian-American organized crime figure in Detroit who became known nationwide because of his role in the disappearance of Jimmy Hoffa in 1975. He was sentenced to 10 years in prison for tax evasion and was involved in the Hotel Gotham numbers racket.

Carlo Gambino (1902-1976): A Sicilian-American crime boss who took over the American Mafia Commission after Vito Genovese's imprisonment in 1959. He was part of a criminal organization led by Joe Masseria. After Genovese's death, Gambino took control of The Commission, which he despised for drug dealing. Gambino's death in 1976 was due to his heart condition and hospitalizations. His legacy continues to be portrayed in the media.

Charles "Lucky" Luciano (1897-1962): He was an Italian-born gangster who was a key figure in establishing the Commission in 1931 and organized crime in the United States. He was a key aide in Joe Masseria's criminal organization and was involved in the Castellammarese War, a rivalry between Masseria and Salvatore Maranzano. Luciano controlled lucrative criminal rackets in New York City and proposed a national Commission to settle disputes. In 1936, he was convicted of compulsory prostitution. His sentence was 30 to 50 years in prison. He was deported to Italy in 1946.

The Commission: Established in 1931 by Charles "Lucky" Luciano, was responsible for overseeing all Mafia activities in the United States and mediating conflicts among families. It consisted of seven family bosses, including New York's Five Families, Chicago Outfit boss Al Capone, and Buffalo family boss Stefano Magaddino. The Commission faced challenges, including the Apalachin meeting in 1957, a plot to kill members in 1963, and the Mafia Commission Trial in 1985. Luciano was convicted of being part of the "Combination" prostitution ring and sentenced to 30-50 years in state prison. The Commission's current membership consists of the Five Families and the Chicago Outfit.

Francis Joseph Sheeran (1920-2003): Often known as "The Irishman," Sheeran was a labor union official in the United States and an enforcer for Jimmy Hoffa and Russell Bufalino. He was suspected of having ties to the Bufalino criminal family and being engaged in organized crime infiltration into unions. In 1980,

Sheeran was convicted of labor racketeering and sentenced to 13 years in jail. Before he died in 2003, he confessed to having assassinated Teamster leader Jimmy Hoffa. His story served as the inspiration for Martin Scorsese's 2019 film The Irishman.

Frank Costello (1891-1973): He was an Italian-American crime boss who was part of the Luciano crime family. Born in 1891, he joined the Morello gang in the U.S.**U.S.** in 1895. He controlled slot machine and bookmaking operations, bringing millions in profit. Costello faced multiple convictions and was stripped of U.S. citizenship in 1952.

Frank Edward Fitzsimmons (1908-1981): He was an American labor union leader, president of the Teamsters Union from 1971 to 1981, and before that, the acting president from 1967 to 1971. Fitzsimmons had worked as a bus driver and truck driver before joining Teamsters Local 299. He negotiated a national trucking contract and formed the Alliance for Labor Action in 1968. In 1971, Hoffa resigned as president, and Fitzsimmons was elected as international president.

James Riddle Hoffa (1913-1975): An American labor union leader and president of the International Brotherhood of Teamsters from 1957 to 1971. He became involved with organized crime in 1964 and resigned in 1971. Jimmy Hoffa, a Detroit truck driver, played a significant role in the Teamsters Union, defending them from raids and expanding their influence. Hoffa was convicted in 1964 of several charges. He resigned in 1971 but was barred from union activities until 1980. Hoffa disappeared on July 30, 1975, and is generally accepted to be murdered by the Mafia.

John Edgar Hoover (1895-1972): He was an American law-enforcement administrator who served as the final Director of the

Bureau of Investigation and the first Director of the Federal Bureau of Investigation (FBI). Before the Apalachin Meeting, for a long time, he had denied that Mafia existed. He expanded the FBI and modernized policing technology. He was credited with overseeing several captures of outlaws and bank robbers and was credited with investigating Communist subversion and the "Top Hoodlum Program."

John Sciandra (1899-1949): He was the Italian-American crime boss of the Northeastern Pennsylvania crime family from 1933 to 1949. Born in Montedoro, Sicily, he immigrated to the United States in 1908 and worked as a coal miner before becoming an enforcer and bootlegger for Bufalino crime family boss Santo Volpe. In 1933, after being questioned about his involvement in the murder of Samuel Wichner, Santo Volpe appointed Sciandra as the new boss.

Joseph Mario Barbara (1905-1959): Also known as "Joe the Barber," Barbara was an Italian-American mobster who led the Bufalino crime family from 1949 to 1959. Born in Sicily, he worked as a hitman for the Northeastern Pennsylvania crime family and was arrested for multiple murders. In 1944, he bought a property in Apalachin, New York, and was convicted of illegally purchasing sugar. In 1957, he hosted the Apalachin meeting, where over 100 mafiosi discussed gambling, narcotics smuggling, and international narcotics trade.

Mike Rizzitello (1927-2005): He was an Italian-American mobster. He was involved in organized crime and illegal gambling. He served nine years in prison and was banned from casinos in Las Vegas.

Min Matheson (1909-1992): She was a labor union organizer of the International Ladies' Garment Workers Union (ILGWU). She is better known for his intense and fearless union activity in

Northeastern Pennsylvania from 1945 to 1963. Born in Chicago, she faced violence in mafia-controlled labor industries. She joined the ILGWU in 1944 and faced opposition from organized crime bosses. Min contributed to workers' personal lives with education, health benefits, and maternity benefits. She was a founding member of the National Organization for Women, aiming for equal rights for women.

The Rainbow Room: This was a private event space in Midtown Manhattan, New York City, and was a popular destination for the elite and celebrities. Opened in 1934, it was a saloon and dance hall that hosted celebrities and royalty. After a decline in business, it closed in 2009 and reopened in 2014 after renovations. The restaurant was declared a landmark in 2012 and awarded an award for outstanding interior architecture by the American Institute of Architects in 2017. The restaurant features a revolving dance floor inspired by Murray's Roman Gardens and has received positive reviews but is rated as expensive.

Stefano Magaddino (1891-1974): He was an Italian-born Mafia boss of the Buffalo crime family in western New York. He was a charter member of the American Mafia's ruling council, The Commission. Born in Sicily, Magaddino led a clan allied with Giuseppe Bonanno and his brother. He orchestrated the murder of Felice Buccellato in 1917 and was arrested in 1921 for murdering Camillo Caiozzo. Magaddino became a naturalized U.S. citizen in 1924 and made a fortune through several criminal activities like loan-sharking, illegal gambling, extortion, and labor racketeering. He was the longest-tenured boss in the American Mafia's history and was involved in nationwide Cosa Nostra affairs.

The Teamsters: The International Brotherhood of Teamsters is a labor union formed in 1903 by merging the Teamsters International Union and the Teamsters National Union. The union has a decentralized structure, with local unions governing themselves autonomously. Despite corruption during its early years, the IBT has grown significantly, becoming one of the most powerful unions in the country by World War II. The union faced political power struggles during the Great Depression and war, with Dave Beck and Jimmy Hoffa gaining control.

Tony Provenzano (1917-1988): He was a prominent American mobster and member of the Genovese crime family New Jersey faction. Born in 1917, he worked as a business agent and president at Teamsters Local 560 in Union City, New Jersey. Provenzano was indicted for extortion in 1963 and served four and a half years in prison. He was also indicted for conspiracy to violate the anti-kickback statute and sentenced to life imprisonment.

William "Mafia's Big Billy" D'Elia (1946): He was an American former mobster who was the boss of the Bufalino crime family after the death of Russell Bufalino in 1994. He grew up in Pittston, Pennsylvania, and worked with the family as a driver and gofer. After Bufalino's death, D'Elia tried to expand the family's activities, including money laundering. In 1990, he was implicated in a money laundering operation involving The Metro newspaper. D'Elia was indicted in 2008 on money laundering and cooperated with law enforcement.

Umberto "Albert" Anastasia (1902-1957): An Italian-American mobster and crime boss who founded the American Mafia and co-founded Murder, Inc. He controlled New York City's waterfront and was known as The Earthquake, The One-Man Army, Mad

Hatter, and Lord High Executioner. Anastasia was part of the Luciano crime family and was involved in the murder of Morris Diamond and Peter Panto. Genovese sought control of Anastasia's family but was indicted on narcotics trafficking charges.

Vito Genovese (1897-1969): He was an Italian-born American mobster who rose to power during Prohibition and played a significant role in the American Mafia. He was a childhood friend of Lucky Luciano and played a role in the Castellammarese War, shaping organized crime in the United States. Genovese served as a mentor to Vincent "Chin" Gigante and later led Luciano's crime family, which was renamed the Genovese crime family in his honor. Genovese was convicted on narcotics conspiracy charges, and in 1959, he was sentenced to 15 years in prison. Genovese died in prison in 1969 and is buried in Saint John Cemetery in Middle Village, Queens.

REFERENCES

Beck L. (2019, November 28). *What happened to the Bufalino crime family from the Irishman?* Refinery 29. https://www.refinery29.com/en-us/2019/11/8643809/where-is-the-bufalino-crime-family-now-the-irishman#:~:text=According%20to%20the%20Times%20Leader

Birkbeck M. (2013). *The quiet Don: The untold story of mafia kingpin Russell Bufalino.* New York: Berkley Books.

Birkbeck M. (2023, July 8). *The real mafia was more involved in 'The Godfather' than anyone knew.* New York Post. https://nypost.com/2023/07/08/the-real-mafia-was-incredibly-involved-in-the-godfather/

Bruney G. (2019, November 27). *Russell Bufalino took the true story of the Irishman to his grave.* Esquire. https://www.esquire.com/entertainment/movies/a29961398/russell-bufalino-the-irishman-true-story/

Corsino, L. (2014). *The neighborhood outfit: Organized crime in Chicago Heights.* University of Illinois Press. http://www.jstor.org/stable/10.5406/j.ctt6wr6fx

Drapper_Don. (2011, July 17). *The Bufalino file: A look inside the massive FBI paper trail on NEPA's most notorious mobster.* Five Families of New York City.

http://www.fivefamiliesnyc.com/2011/07/bufalino-file-look-inside-massive-fbi.html

Hayes A. (2022, December 3). *Bootleggers, bathtub gin, & speakeasies: Organized crime in the 1920s.* The Collector. https://www.thecollector.com/organized-crime-roaring-twenties/

Role of the internal revenue service in law enforcement activities: Hearings before the Subcommittee on administrations of the internal revenue code of the committee on finance United States Senate, 94th Cong. (1975, 1976). https://bit.ly/3PCOSYy

Cheney J. (2023, April 10). *Exploring Scranton's Industrial History at the Anthracite Heritage Museum.* History in Northeastern Pennsylvania Archives. https://uncoveringpa.com/anthracite-heritage-museum

Krainc. A.E. (2022, March 10). *Prohibition & organized crime in the 1920s.* Study.com. https://study.com/learn/lesson/prohibition-organized-crime-1920s-history-aftermath.html

Lubasch A.H. (1977, October 22). *Bufalino sentenced on extortion charge.* The New York Times. https://www.nytimes.com/1977/10/22/archives/bufalino-sentenced-on-extortion-charge-reputed-mobster-gets-four.html

Lubasch A.H. (1981, October 21). *Trial of 2 crime figures told of plot to kill key witness.* The New York Times. https://www.nytimes.com/1981/10/21/nyregion/trial-of-2-crime-figures-told-of-plot-to-kill-key-witness.html

McBride J. (2022, October 11). *Bufalino crime family now & then: Does it exist today?* Heavy.com.

https://heavy.com/entertainment/2019/11/bufalino-crime-family-today-now/

Organized crime in America: Hearings before the Committee on the Judiciary United States Senate. 98th Cong. (1983).
https://www.ojp.gov/pdffiles1/Digitization/92732NCJRS.pdf

Kaiser, D. (2008). *The toad to Dallas: The assassination of John F. Kennedy.* Harvard University Press.
https://doi.org/10.2307/j.ctt13x0j3v

Pennsylvania Crime Commission (1970). *Report on organized crime.* The American Mafia. https://mafiahistory.us/maf-pcc70.html

Pennsylvania Crime Commission (1989). *Report on organized crime.* Commonwealth of Pennsylvania.
https://www.ojp.gov/pdffiles1/Digitization/138666NCJRS.pdf

Pennsylvania Historical & Museum Commission. (2015, August 26). *1861-1945: Era of industrial ascend*ancy. Pennsylvania Historical & Museum Commission.
http://www.phmc.state.pa.us/portal/communities/pa-history/1861-1945.html

Serratore A. (2019, November 21). *The true history behind Martin Scorsese's 'The Irishman'.* Smithsonian Magazine.
https://www.smithsonianmag.com/history/truth-behind-martin-scorseses-irishman-180973620/

Sokol T. (2019, November 29). *The Irishman: Real life gangsters from Philly and New York.* Den of Geek.
https://www.denofgeek.com/culture/the-irishman-real-life-gangsters-history/

Tonry M., & Reuter P. (2020). *Organizing crime: Mafias, markets, and networks*. Chicago and London: The University of Chicago Press.

Valin E. (n.d.). *In Pittston, informing runs in the family*. The American Mafia. https://mafiahistory.us/rattrap/inflatorre.html

Waring E., & David Weisburd (2018). *Crime and social organization: Advances in criminological theory*. Routledge.

Wintermute, B. A. (2017). Crime and Punishment in Eastern Pennsylvania, 1903–18, Part 1. *Pennsylvania History: A Journal of Mid-Atlantic Studies, 84(3)*, 363–385. https://doi.org/10.5325/pennhistory.84.3.0363

Wolensky R. P. (2014). Organizing ladies' garment workers in Northeastern Pennsylvania: Min Matheson and the ILGWU. *Pennsylvania Legacies, 14(1)*, 20–25. https://doi.org/10.5215/pennlega.14.1.0020

Wright, C. (2019). The life and times of Jimmy Hoffa. *Class, Race and Corporate Power, 7(2)*. https://www.jstor.org/stable/48645445

www.ingramcontent.com/pod-product-compliance
Lightning Source LLC
Chambersburg PA
CBHW071355080526
44587CB00017B/3110